Conseco Fieldhouse

THE FIRST YEAR

Conseco Fieldhouse

THE FIRST YEAR

1999-2000

Greetings from the Fieldhouse

Pacers Sports & Entertainment
INDIANAPOLIS, INDIANA

Acknowledgements

Show Promoters/Agents

Editor:	Jeff Johnson
Book Designer:	Jack W. Davis
Writers:	Rick Morwick (Conseco Fieldhouse and Indiana Pacers) Tom Savage (Indiana Fever)
Photographers:	Ron Hoskins, Tim Hursley, Frank McGrath, NBA Photos, SKY-KAM Aerial Photography
Printer:	Sport Graphics
Architect:	Ellerbe Becket Architects & Engineers
Indiana Pacers Communications Department:	David Benner, Tim Edwards, MaryKay Hruskocy, Kathy Jordan, Jeff McCoy, Tom Savage, Julie Spychalski

Copyright

Apregan Entertainment (Neil Diamond)
Arch Angels Music Concerts, Inc.
Artists & Audience Entertainment
Awsome Productions (WCW)
Basketball Sports Marketing (Nike Hoop Summit)
Belkin Productions
Big Ten
Borman Entertainment (Faith Hill)
Calm Before the Storm Foundation
Cellar Door of Michigan
Columbia Artists Management, Inc.
Concerts West
Creative Artists, Inc.
Elton John Management, LTD
Evolution Talent Agency
Famous Artists Agency
Feld Entertainment
Fresh Entertainment
Goliath Talent Agency (Master P)
Harlem Globetrotters
Haymon Entertainment
Heartland Film Festival
Heritage Keepers
Hoffman Entertainment (Mellencamp)
IMC
Indiana Black Expo
Indiana High School Athletic Association
Indiana University
Intersport, Inc.
John Landau Management (Bruce Springsteen)
M. & M Sports, Inc.
Magicworks
Metropolitan Entertainment
Monterey Peninsula Artists
Moore Entertainment
National Association of Basketball Coaches
North Central High School
OK Visions (Sarah Brightman)
Park Place Entertainment (Boxing)
Peter Lowe Agency
Premier Productions
Principal Artists Group (Ricky Martin)
Purdue University
QBQ Entertainment
RPM Management (Tim McGraw)
Rudas Organization
SFX/Sunshine
The Firm (Backstreet Boys, Kiss & Limp Bizkie)
The Howard Rose Agency
The Indianapolis Star
The Promotion Company
Tin Pan Apple Productions (Dr. Dre)
Titan Sports, Inc..
TNA
Tom Collins Enterprises
Uppercut Management (Kid Rock)
Varnell Enterprises
W.A.C. Entertainment/Pate
Warren Central High School
William Morris Agency
World Championship Wrestling

Photo Credits

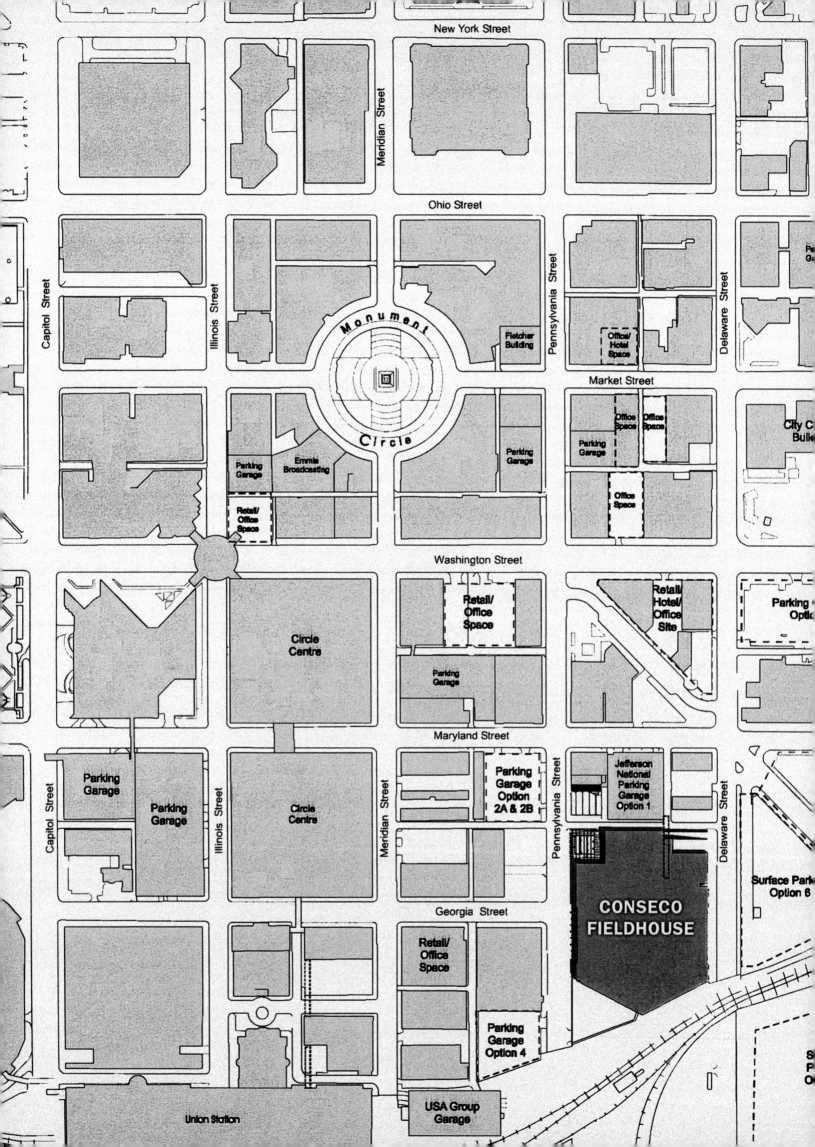

Contents

Introduction

I remember on July 22, 1997, putting a shovel into some dirt and thinking, "This is really going to happen." I don't think, up to a certain point, many people thought it would happen. But it did.

I always thought we could get Conseco Fieldhouse built. But I knew when I talked about it for the first time it was a pipe dream. I also felt it was necessary to put in the minds of different groups of people in the city because I understood how important it was going to be down the road, both to the city and the franchise.

From that point, the Indiana Pacers started becoming very successful and I think some of the things pointed out in those meetings started to become evident and that really started the ball rolling. I do remember not many people really giving us a chance to get a building. But we got an awful lot of help from different people, such as the Capitol Improvement Board, a task force that was assembled for the building, former Mayor Stephen Goldsmith, former Governor Evan Bayh and current Governor Frank O'Bannon, to name a few.

From a practical standpoint, Conseco Fieldhouse allows us to go forward in the NBA and be financially responsible in a competitive way against the rest of the league. Beyond the basketball, when you have a building like this, I think it's important it goes past the tradition that it represents. It has become a great assembly hall for some major events and will continue to be a gathering place for our community for a wide variety of events. I think The Fieldhouse has an unlimited future as far as the great

events that will be held here and we've already started scheduling those kinds of events, such as the 2002 World Basketball Championships, the 2004 Olympic Wrestling Trials, and the 2004 World Short Course Swimming Championships. This is an indication that this is another venue in the city of Indianapolis that will draw the biggest events in the world.

Today, as president of Pacers Sports & Entertainment, I look at Conseco Fieldhouse with many different feelings. First and foremost, I'm extremely proud of what it represents in a spiritual way, which is the great tradition and history of basketball in this state. We tried to embody that in the building and I think we accomplished it.

Then I think of all the people involved, who have made The Fieldhouse the special place that it is: the fans, who sold out the building for every Pacers' home game through the regular season and the playoffs, making this the most difficult place to play in the National Basketball Association.

I also think of the citizens of Indianapolis, Indiana and from across the country who visited Conseco Fieldhouse for basketball games, other sporting events, concerts, family entertainment, conventions, seminars or assemblies of people, and those who made the building a reality, from our owners, Herb and Mel Simon, to the employees of Pacers Sports & Entertainment to government officials to architects to construction workers.

When you look back on a project like this, there are so many people who played a role and that's what makes Conseco Fieldhouse more unique than its design and one-of-a-kind look. It is not anyone's building, it is everyone's building.

This book is a reflection of that. From the shovel of dirt to Opening Night, November 6, 1999, and the tribute to Indiana's 50 Greatest Basketball Players. And then to a year that saw a wide variety of entertainment, it seems so long ago because it went by so quickly.

As you look through this book, we hope the pace slows somewhat as you reflect on the many special moments of Conseco Fieldhouse in its first year. Even if you weren't in attendance for some or all of the events, please share the photos and accompanying text as if you were. It was a special year, filled with special memories.

I have many of those. Seeing the Pacers reach the NBA Finals for the first time stands out, as does Opening Night when we had the tribute to Indiana's 50 Greatest Basketball Players, including the final trio at center court—Larry Bird, Oscar Robertson and John Wooden. That was somewhat of a defining moment because it represented our goal of trying to become part of the tradition of Indiana basketball. It was overwhelming to look at this building and to think because of the Pacers, we've established a building in the city of Indianapolis that represents in every way the great feeling people here have about basketball.

As we reflect, we will also look ahead. As far as I'm concerned, construction isn't completed in Conseco Fieldhouse. It is missing an NBA Championship banner and I will do my best to try to provide a team capable of applying that finishing touch.

Meanwhile, please enjoy what we have experienced and what we will experience. If the future of the Fieldhouse is anything like its first year, we all have a lot to look forward to.

Sincerely,

Donnie Walsh
President, Pacers Sports & Entertainment

Conseco Fieldhouse

It is only fitting that the world's finest basketball venue is nestled in the heart of the basketball capital of the world.

Indiana is, after all, the world's basketball cradle and is home to the sport's most passionate fans. And because the state's professional team, the Indiana Pacers, plays in downtown Indianapolis, what better place to erect a basketball shrine like Conseco Fieldhouse?

Bottom line: there is no better place.

Because in Indiana, basketball is more than just a game. Much more.

"....We tried to make it the finest basketball arena in the country...."

Conseco "Quotes"

Philadelphia 76ers Coach Larry Brown on Conseco Fieldhouse: "This is the greatest place. This is what a basketball arena is supposed to be like. There is so much charm here."
INDIANAPOLIS STAR
2/8

It is a hallowed institution. And fans embrace its tradition-steeped legacy, which encompasses its high school, college and professional teams alike, like a dear friend.

Nowhere on earth is basketball more appreciated and revered than in Indiana. So quite naturally, nowhere on earth is there a more majestic spectator facility than the 18,345-seat Conseco Fieldhouse, which enters its second season of operation as the stylistically unique home of the Indiana Pacers and the WNBA Indiana Fever.

"It's important for our fans to come to a building that is on a par or better than those being built or that have been built in the United States," Pacers Sports & Entertainment President Donnie Walsh said. "It's unique. We tried to make it the finest basketball arena in the country.

"We've had the advantage of looking at the new arenas that have been built and taking the best out of those arenas."

In the end, however, the city did not build a mere arena. It built an edifice far superior.

It built a fieldhouse. Or rather, The Fieldhouse.

Cutting-edge and retro, state-of-the-art and nostalgic, Conseco Fieldhouse was constructed on the model of Indiana's old high school and college "fieldhouses," where standing-room only crowds were the norm on any given wintry Friday nights.

In design and concept, Conseco Fieldhouse, the only fieldhouse in the NBA, pays tribute to the state's storied basketball past while providing the finest comfort and luxury accommodations to fans.

In short, visitors do not simply visit Conseco Fieldhouse.

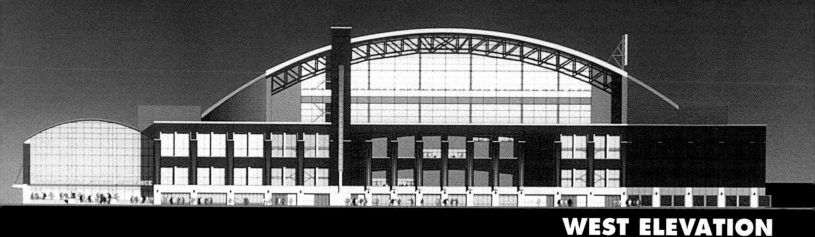

They experience it.

"It's nice for the fans," said former Pacers coach and Indiana legend Larry Bird, who led the team to its first-ever trip to the NBA Finals last season. "You don't build arenas for players, you build them for fans.

"I think it's the finest one in the league, and I think our fans enjoy it, and it's something we are proud of."

Bird is correct on all counts.

Experts from around the world agree that the Fieldhouse is not only the finest facility in the NBA, it is the finest basketball building anywhere — period. Pacers' players, coaches and front office executives adore the structure, and, as evidenced by the fact that for the first time in franchise history the Pacers sold out all 41 home games, fans love it, too.

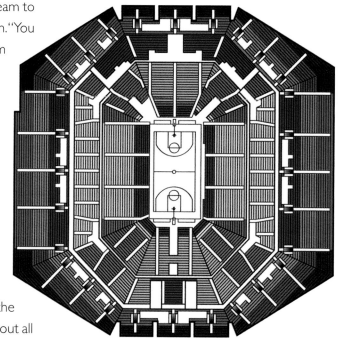

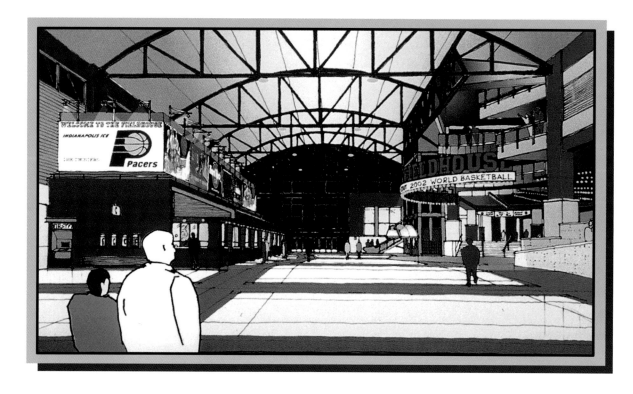

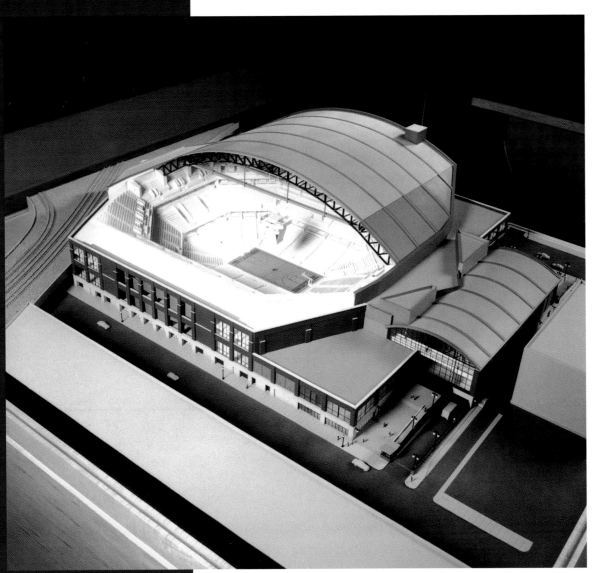

NBC's Bob Costas
said Conseco
Fieldhouse "is winning
raves all around the
league, many think
it's the best building
in the NBA."
(Opening of Game 4
during the NBA Finals)

Herb Simon, Indiana Pacers Owner, addresses media during the ground breaking ceremonies on July 22, 1997.

''We think we've been able to capture the history of Indiana basketball, the cultural importance it has played in this state and yet be able to stand up and say, 'Nobody has done this before,'' PS&E General Manager David Kahn said. ''We did not want this to be the last of this generation of sports buildings.

''We wanted to be the first of the next generation.''

By all indications, The Fieldhouse concept is the paradigm for future projects.

Greetings from the Fieldhouse

17

(L to R)

Herb Simon, Indiana Pacers Owner;

Stephen Goldsmith, Former Mayor of Indianapolis;

Donnie Walsh, President of Pacers Sports & Entertainment;

Stephen Hilbert, Former Chairman and CEO of Conseco.

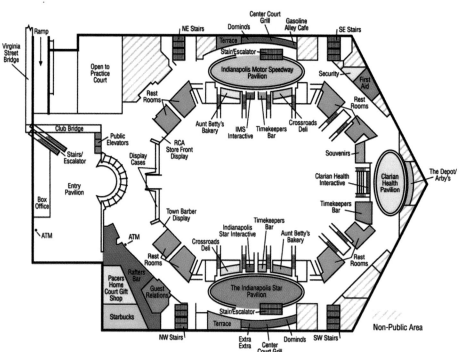

THE BEGINNING

Prior to last season, the Pacers played in Market Square Arena, which opened in 1974. Popular and cozy, MSA was the site of many magical Pacers moments — especially in the 1990s, when Indiana evolved into a perennial NBA power.

Capacity crowds bestowed upon MSA the well-deserved label of being home to the NBA's Loudest Sixth Man. The Pacers loved playing in MSA because they routinely fed off the raucous energy of adoring fans who cheered at a fever pitch from the opening-tip to the final horn.

It was Hoosier Hysteria at its finest.

Yet, despite the distinct homecourt advantage the Pacers had in MSA, the facility was not without its drawbacks — especially for fans, who had an increasingly difficult time navigating its narrow corridors and accessing increasingly jammed concession stands and restrooms, which were too small and sparse. The arena's seats were also small and uncomfortable.

In addition, MSA was not altogether fan-friendly in that the majority of seats were in the upper bowl, not the lower. It also had no luxury suites — a standard in today's new arenas.

And last but not least, the building itself lacked charm and character. Apart from the game itself being played on the court, MSA's surroundings were static. The building, which seated less than 17,000, was simply a place to watch a game and little more.

So when it was finally determined that the Pacers needed a better home, the new facility was designed strictly with fans in mind. And planners

The first family event at Conseco Fieldhouse was the "75th Anniversary Show for Disney on Ice." The show featured nine performances running December 1-5, 1999.

Over 1,200 workers
were needed to build
Conseco Fieldhouse.

Jess Stump, Pacers season ticket holder,
enjoys the view from the Club Seat level where
he's already reserved his seats.

Greetings from Conseco Fieldhouse

couldn't think of a better way to excite fans than
with a magnificent new building that paid homage
to the state's glorious basketball tradition and, at
the same time, provide a spacious spectating
environment teeming with all the amenities
one might expect in a trend-setting 21st century arena.

"I think it culminates all of our dreams for the
Pacers, but I think it also encompasses everything that is Indiana basketball to me," said
Walsh, who, along with Kahn, was among the
project's chief visionaries. "That was our goal
when we started this, and I'm talking about
when we started back in 1986 to build a
team.

"We wanted the team to be a part of the
tradition of Indiana basketball, which it really hadn't
been up until that point in the NBA. It has been a
long process over many years, but I think it culminates with Conseco Fieldhouse because it embod-
ies it."

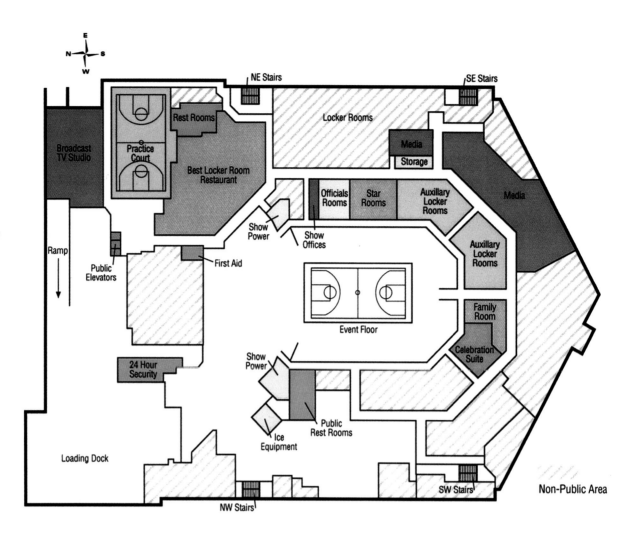

NE Stairs

SE Stairs

Broadcast TV Studio

Practice Court

Rest Rooms

Locker Rooms

Media

Storage

Best Locker Room Restaurant

Officials Rooms

Star Rooms

Auxiliary Locker Rooms

Media

Show Power

Show Offices

Auxiliary Locker Rooms

Ramp

Public Elevators

First Aid

Event Floor

Family Room

Celebration Suite

24 Hour Security

Show Power

Ice Equipment

Public Rest Rooms

Loading Dock

SW Stairs

Non-Public Area

NW Stairs

Conseco Fieldhouse occupies more than 750,000 square feet, which is nearly triple that of Market Square Arena.

Ground breaking on Conseco Fieldhouse was on July 22, 1997.

BREAKING GROUND

Funding for the Fieldhouse was created through a partnership of private and public financing. And it was done so without a general tax increase to the public.

Rather, funding was derived from a three-party partnership that included the Pacers; local corporations; and the public through a special tax district that recycles state revenues for investments in civic projects.

With funding for the $183 million project secured, Governor Frank O'Bannon, then-Indianapolis Mayor Stephen Goldsmith, Pacers owners Mel and Herb Simon and Walsh took up silver shovels and took part in a ceremonial ground-breaking on July 22, 1997.

"This project cleared some serious stumbling blocks," Goldsmith said. "And it's only by the determination and hard work of many in the community that we were able to gather for the ground-breaking ceremony."

"What will be built will be a major city asset that residents throughout Indiana will be able to enjoy for many years."

And for more reasons than just basketball.

In reality, Conseco Fieldhouse is much more than just a basketball arena. It is a multi-purpose entertainment center that offers something for just about everyone.

The Fieldhouse is a place for concerts, ice shows, circuses and so on. And it can be reconfigured to host other sporting events, such as swimming and ice hockey. Lending the city a distinct edge in attracting major entertainment events and national and international athletic competitions that otherwise would overlook Indianapolis had the Fieldhouse not been built.

Former Chairman and CEO of Conseco, Stephen Hilbert, and Indiana Pacers Owner, Herb Simon, unveil the new logo of Conseco Fieldhouse.

CONSECO FIELDHOUSE—THE FIRST YEAR

IT'S HALFTIME

Greetings from Conseco Fieldhouse

THE DESIGN

Beyond simply building an arena where fans would feel comfortable watching a game, the Pacers wanted something else — charm.

Planners desperately wanted to avoid the trend of constructing massive, soul-less structures that were built for professional sports teams during the 1970s and '80s.

"I think there are places in the NBA or elsewhere in basketball that have feeling and atmosphere, whatever you want to call it, and then there are buildings that are big, sterile buildings you just play in," Walsh said. "We wanted this building to have a special feeling to it, that when people came into it, they felt part of the tradition the building is for."

To find that "feel," Kahn traveled extensively across the country, examining new and old basketball and baseball stadiums — including Baltimore's pristine Camden Yards — and comparing and contrasting the charms of each facility.

What he liked, he committed to memory. What he didn't, he discarded.

"I saw some that were done wonderfully and some that were done all right and some that, whether due to budget or whatever, were done on a so-so basis," Kahn said.

"I'm convinced after seeing them all that this will stand on its own as the best in the business. I think that everybody in the NBA and everybody who is a basketball fan will be talking about this building for years to come."

Why?

Because it's one-of-a-kind in every aspect, from its stunning outside beauty to its breathtaking opulence on the inside.

Erected in the heart of downtown's southeast side historic Wholesale District, the Fieldhouse sports a distinct red brick and steel exterior. A semi-barrel-shaped roof and rows of windows beneath encircle the entire structure, which is located just a few blocks south of MSA.

By design of Ellerbe Becket, the lead architect on the project, it looks like a fieldhouse, not an arena. And by design, the interior is distinctly un-arena-like, as well. It is pristine, palatial and sprawling.

The entry pavilion alone is a sight to behold.

Encompassing 16,000 square feet, the entry pavilion features an old-fashioned box office with 18 ticket windows. It is open to the public during non-event times and has a majestic view into the seating bowl and the adjoining practice court.

It also provides access to the team store, which itself covers 10,000 square feet, making it the largest of its kind in the NBA.

In total, the Fieldhouse occupies 750,000 square feet on 6.2 acres. It has 71 private suites and it features 2,500 club seats.

Dotted throughout the building are concession and novelty stands, restaurants, a team store and — as testimony to the Fieldhouse's uniqueness and emphasis on fun — a store crafted to look like a turn-of-the-century barber shop where fans can have

Club Seats—An EXCELLENT View of the Action!

Exclusive Club Restaurant

Greetings from the Fieldhouse

their faces painted. Next to the barber shop is a deli counter, along with an interactive video arcade, which are but a sampling of the many treats and experiences the Fieldhouse has to offer — not the least of which are the building's wider corridors, which makes touring the facility a far easier endeavor than it was at MSA.

For example, the narrowest part of Conseco Fieldhouse is 24 feet, which is considerably wider than MSA's widest part, which was 18 feet.

As Bird said, "You don't build arenas for players, you build them for fans."

Another breathtaking feature is the Grand Staircase leading to the extra-wide main-level brick concourse that is adorned with trophy and memorabilia cases that meander through three main pavilions.

And speaking of the pavilions, each contains displays that serve as paeans to the state's rich basketball, health and auto racing traditions. A stroll through each pavilion is, for some, like a stroll down Memory Lane. For visitors of a younger generation, it is an enlightening peek back to Indiana's Golden Age, with images similar to those captured in the classic 1986 Hollywood film "Hoosiers."

Enhancing the nostalgic feel is the fact there are no back-lit advertisements in the Fieldhouse. The signs are all front-lit neon or hand-painted murals — just like the good old days, when basketball was king and the fieldhouses were castles.

"The experience in the winter in Indiana is basketball," said Walsh, a native New Yorker who is keenly aware and enamored of the state's love affair with the game. "You can draw on that, and that feeling was exactly what we were looking for.

"It's a big part of the culture here. I've never been to a place where it's quite like here."

As if the pavilions and main entry level weren't spectacular enough, the seating bowl itself is a marvel all its own.

Rising 15 stories into the Indianapolis skyline, the bowl features a fieldhouse ceiling that slopes in an arch and is supported by exposed steel beams.

Did You Know?

Over 2,600 tons of steel was used to construct the arching dome of Conseco Fieldhouse.

Giant glass windows rim the top of the east and west arches, which let in sunlight and are visually appealing.

As for seating, the Fieldhouse is divided into five tiers — three levels of seating that sandwich two levels of suites. The theater-style seats are hunter green and 20 inches wide — an inch wider than those at MSA.

There is even a section of seats in one end zone that are designed like bleachers, which seat about 225 people and can be rolled in and out just like the old high school and college gyms.

"It has exceeded our expectations."

But most importantly, as the saying goes, there isn't a bad seat in the house.

From the $100 to $300 courtside seats to the $10 upper level seats, the Fieldhouse was built specifically with the viewing pleasure of spectators in mind.

Take the main scoreboard, for example.

Massive but sleek, the four-sided object is laced with neon and can entertain fans with anything ranging from movies to live in-house video to instant replays on four 16-by-9-foot Mitsubishi video screens.

"This is the Camden Yards of basketball," said Rick Fuson, the Fieldhouse's Senior Vice President and Executive Director. "We don't know of anybody else that's done this type of thing in the NBA, and we think it is the first themed building, basketball or multipurpose, with a retro-look, of any in the country.

"It has exceeded our expectations."

The building's splendor even marvels those who conceived and built it.

"I think people will be amazed when they see it," said project manager John Hilkene, who also worked on Washington's MCI Centre and Cleveland's Gund Arena. "You are transported back in time to a 1940s style fieldhouse, but it will still have the updated technology.

Tom Proebstle, project designer for Ellerbe Beckett, agrees. "At the beginning of this project, we wanted to develop a mantra that would be the guiding light into a successful project," Proebstle said. "The mantra we developed is, 'A Fieldhouse for the 21st century."

The Clarian Heath Pavilion is one of three sponsor pavilions on the Main Concourse of Conseco Fieldhouse. The pavilion features a wide variety of concessions and an interactive area with a life-size Operation Game.

"Our charge from the Pacers' organization was to create a themed environment that will do for basketball what the retro-styled stadiums have done for baseball. We took it a step further, carrying the theme all the way to the advertising on the walls and the food being served in the concession stands."

The point that can't be overstated is: The creators thought of everything, from creature comforts, to bistro-style dining, to old-fashioned concessions, to aesthetic constructs to unparalleled accessibility for persons with disabilities.

In fact, the Fieldhouse has already won an award for its excellence in that area.

"This building was built with everyone in mind, not just the corporate partners who take advantage of the suites and sponsorship opportunities, but also loyal season-ticket holders and fans," Kahn said. "Sightlines, no matter where you sit, have been engineered for basketball and the experience of the NBA."

Located on the Balcony Level, the Finish Line Pavilion features everyone's favorite concessions. Here you can check out the display of high school basketball teams and memorabilia from the movie "Hoosiers."

CONSECO FIELDHOUSE — THE FIRST YEAR

JUST THE FACTS

Amenities, amenities. You'll find no shortage in the Fieldhouse.

Here's a quick look at what makes the building unique and what it has to offer.

- 103 permanent points of concession sale and 37 mobile units.
- 560 restroom fixtures, more than double that of MSA.
- 33 water fountains, compared to 18 at MSA.
- 750,000 square feet, compared to 290,000 at MSA.
- Three automatic teller machines.
- Adjoining practice court, the only one of its kind in the NBA that is viewable to fans from the street.
- Four truck doors.
- Three first aid stations.
- Three escalators.
- Two guest service stations.

Those are the hard facts. Here are some fun facts about how the Fieldhouse was built.

- More than 2,600 tons of steel went into the arching dome.
- The building contains 58,000 square feet of glass.
- Approximately 600,000 bricks and 550,000 concrete blocks were in the construction of the facility.
- Roughly 38,000 miles of cable were used during construction.
- And last, but by no means least, more than 1,200 jobs were created over the life of the construction.

Much of the advertising on display in Conseco Fieldhouse is hand painted signs located in the concourses. There are more than 40 hand painted signs in Conseco Fieldhouse.

"This is the best facility in our league."

And further good news for the city is, the amount of permanent new jobs that were created — or that might still be created — are countless because of construction of the Fieldhouse, which can't help but lure visitors by the thousands to downtown.

"We know that entertainment hospitality is the largest job-generator in Center Township (greater Indianapolis)," former mayor Goldsmith said. "What we're doing is investing a number of dollars that the city would never have otherwise had in order to build an important facility that will bring over two million people to downtown Indianapolis."

After one full season in their new home, during which time the Pacers sold out every game and advanced to the NBA Finals for the very first time, the Fieldhouse appears to be an unqualified success story.

"I've been to all the buildings in the NBA," Kahn said. "This is the best facility in our league."

"No other NBA building is a throwback, a retro. Everything has been done with a detailed, loving approach to make it feel like the old high school and college fieldhouses of the 1940s and 50s."

NEW HOME

Fully furnished, 750,000 sq. ft. downtown showplace, large living room, seats 18,500.

Call 317-917-2500 for information

See You There!

PLAYERS LOVE IT, TOO

As Bird asserts, arenas are built for fans and their comfort and enjoyment. But that doesn't mean that players can't enjoy them, too. And in the Fieldhouse, there is plenty for players to love — from the plush, spacious locker rooms to the state-of-the-art training room to the extraordinarily equipped weight room to the one-of-a-kind adjoining practice court that is viewable to pedestrians on Delaware Street. "I felt at home at Conseco Fieldhouse pretty much right away," said veteran center Rik Smits, who has spent all 12 of his NBA seasons with the Pacers "I really haven't missed Market Square Arena for one second." At MSA, the players' quarters were cramped, to say the least. Barely large enough for 15 NBA athletes to maneuver around with any degree of comfort, conditions became downright claustrophobic when reporters flowed in for post-game interviews.

JIM L CANADY III
86-89 PACEMATES

DICK MONTIETH
WON THE GAME

THE TOWLES
FAMILY

PRIN
-RAND

GLYNN JOHNSON
INGERSOLL-RAND

INGERSOLL-RAND INGERSOLL-RAND

The Pacers Foundation provided a unique opportunity to purchase bricks used in the construction of the interior of Conseco Fieldhouse. This area, known as the Thomas W. Binford Friends of the Foundation Memorial Wall, honors the charter board member and one of Indianapolis' most influential men.

This special memorial wall is located on the Main Concourse, between the Indianapolis Star and Clarian Heath Pavilions. The bricks are inscribed with more than just names — it is a message that will echo through Conseco Fieldhouse for years to come.

By comparison, the locker rooms at the Fieldhouse are spacious and luxurious.

But most important, everything the Pacers need — be it a training room or a stand-alone practice court — is under one roof. "You have the luxury of always being in the same place," forward Austin Croshere said. "Having one locker room and one training room, there is nothing that you need that isn't here.

"I don't think you really saw anything negative (at MSA) because you didn't know any different. But I think now, if we were to have to drive somewhere else to practice…we're kind of

spoiled with how good things are. This is great."

And let's not forget the amenities.

In addition to the more luxurious locker room facility, the Fieldhouse provides players the very best in what professional athletes require to maintain health and conditioning.

There is a hot tub. There is a cold tub. There is a whirlpool. There is a steam room. There is a sauna. And last but certainly not least, there is a space-age

underwater treadmill that dramatically speeds a player's rehabilitation after being injured.

The treadmill can run up to eight miles per hour and features water jets that players can adjust to provide whatever degree of resistance their rehabilitation requires. And it is equipped with an underwater camera that assists players in doing exercises correctly. "What we've done here is invested in the welfare of the players," said David Craig, the Pacers' head trainer since 1970. "It's their home. They'll have access to it 24 hours a day. If they want to come in and put up a few shots, watch videos, lift weights or just relax, it's their clubhouse. "We wouldn't have built Conseco Fieldhouse if it wasn't for the success of these players. We want to take care of them." At every level, the Fieldhouse meets and — in most instances exceeds — players' needs.

"This place is just the ultimate," Bird said. "It's out of control. This building is built for the Indiana Pacers." That's why they love it.

"It's magnificent," veteran forward Chris Mullin said. "It's geared totally toward basketball. That's a big advantage. It's got a tight feel. It doesn't feel as big as it is. It's like a good, broken-in gym. "Spectacular. Best in the business. It's so unique, there's nothing like it. It's got the old feel with all the amenities, so it's the best of both worlds."

Forward Jalen Rose agrees.

"It's amazing. It's like playing in the Taj Mahal," Rose said. "Growing up, it was a crate with two long sticks with a wooden basket, with the basket nailed into the wood, chain nets. And now, this. "It's great progress, and I'm so excited to be a part of it." So is Pacers' star Reggie Miller, who was initially concerned

The ATA Pavilion is located on the Balcony Level on the west side of the Fieldhouse. In addition to all their favorite food and drinks, fans can test their skills in the ATA skee ball interactive area.

that the new building would not generate as much fan energy and excitement as the famously loud MSA.

But as Miller soon found out, he needn't have worried. "Whether you're a basketball player, a hockey player, ice skater, circus performer, rock star, rap star, opera star, wrestler or whatever, you'll want to be your best because this is the best," said Miller, the Pacers' career-scoring leader and the NBA's all-time leader in 3-point field goals. "A building's reputation can enhance a performance. I think once everyone sees it, what went into it, how unique it is, they'll want to play their best game, put on their best show, leave a lasting memory for the fans. I'm thrilled I get a chance to do just that." Fresh off their first-ever trip to the NBA Finals, the Pacers

next objective is to thrill their fans with a championship banner to adorn their charming new home.

"Hopefully," Rose said, "this is something we can bring to the new arena."

SIMPLY THE BEST

Conseco Fieldhouse is the world's best sports spectator venue because nothing but the best was invested in its design and construction. With a roof 15 stories high, the world's largest crane was brought in to install tresses on top of the building. The machine was so massive that it was disassembled before being moved to the work site and was reassembled on the ground level inside the Fieldhouse.

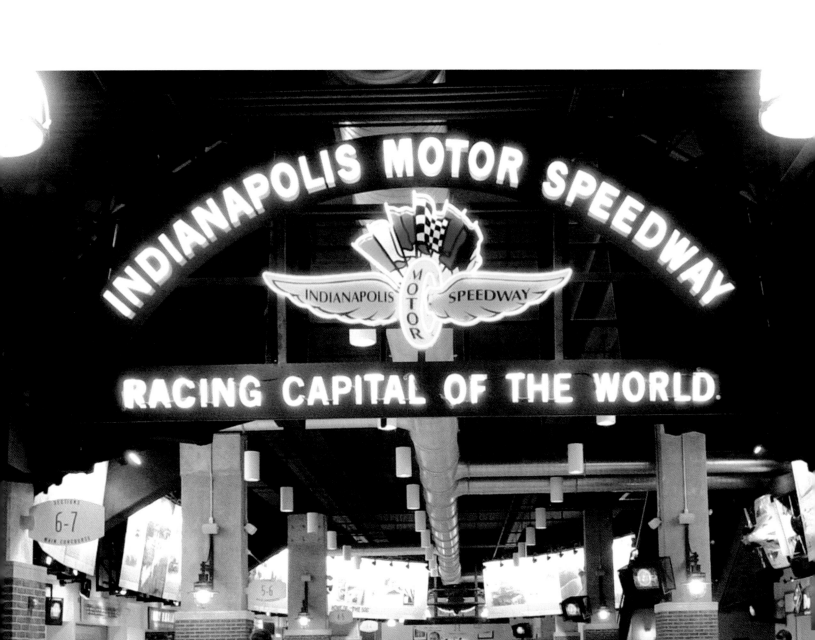

Trace the history of the fabled track in the Indianapolis Motor Speedway Pavilion on the Main Concourse. Fans can look back at past Indianapolis 500 and Brickyard 400 races and peek into the future with Formula One.

This pavilion offers a variety of concessions including a deli, bakery and grill. Also, fans can get behind the wheel of an Indy 500 car and compete against fellow drivers with the virtual Indy Racing Game.

A total 1,200 workers built the structure, which has 600,000 bricks; 550,000 blocks; 660 tons of limestone; 58,000 square feet of glass; and is approximately 170 feet high.

Inside the palatial edifice is the Home Court Team Store, where visitors will find yet another unique marvel: a massive basketball that hangs and rotates just outside the shop.

Weighing in at 3,860 pounds, the basketball is 18 feet across and is made of steel encased with fiberglass. It took 820 man-hours to construct and has 6,870 dimples, which were hand-carved and painted by one craftsman. It also makes one revolution per minute at a 22-degree incline and is powered by a 1/4-horsepower motor.

Fans can enjoy deli, bakery and grill foods or pose for a commemorative photo in the Indianapolis Star Interactive Area.

"....I think people are going to love it...."

The Fieldhouse also offers the best in luxury accommodations for the media — accommodations that include a 2,656-square foot workroom and dining room; four dark rooms for photographers; and two separate rooms reserved exclusively for television interviews.

And again, the Fieldhouse provides the very best in access and convenience for fans with disabilities.

For example, the Fieldhouse has accessible restrooms that include unisex facilities. It also has menus, signage and an accessibility guide in Braille, and a Guest Relations and accessibility coordinator to assist and answer questions.

Again, careful attention to detail was applied to the total design, including the construction, the retro theme, the state-of-the-art technology, the disability access and every creature comfort the Fieldhouse affords all patrons.

"I think that everybody in the NBA and everybody who is a basketball fan will be talking about this building for years to come." So impressed is Walsh with the building that, upon its completion, he found it difficult to find words to accurately reflect his warm affection for the stunningly beautiful Fieldhouse.

"It's...I'm awed," Walsh said. "To see the team out here after all the work it took to put this building together and in place...I think that everyone who worked on it did a great job. It's pretty much down to all the details we put into it. I think people are going to love it when they come in, and I think the building was built for the fans."

"The building, I think, is basically our dream come true. At least, it's mine."

As fans walk the Main Concourse of Conseco Fieldhouse, they can take a stroll through time in the Indianapolis Star Pavilion. Fans can reminisce as they browse large replications of front page sports stories on such topics as Pacers highlights, the 1954 Milan High School State Championship and other basketball moments.

"The building, I think, is basically our dream come true...."

★ November 1999 ★

31	**1**	**2**	**3**	**4**	**5** Blue & Gold Ball	**6** Opening Night Pacers 115 vs. Boston Celtics 108 Ribbon Cutting Ceremony 50 Greatest Players Ceremony
7 Pacers Fan Jam & Indiana Music Festival	**8** WCW Monday Night Nitro	**9**	**10** Bruce Springsteen Concert	**11** Pacers 116 vs. Orlando Magic 101	**12**	**13** Pacers 105 vs. Washington Wizards 83
14 An Evening With Bill Cosby	**15**	**16** Peter Lowe Seminar	**17**	**18**	**19** Pacers 99 vs. Atlanta Hawks 105	**20** Ice 3 vs. San Antonio Iguanas 2
21	**22**	**23**	**24**	**25** Pacers 99 vs. Detroit Pistons 107	**26** Pacers 105 vs. Vancouver Grizzlies 86	**27** Ice 4 vs. Oklahoma City Blazers 5 Pre-Game Christian Concert w/ Newsboys
28	**29**	**30**	**1**	**2**	**3**	**4**

★ December 1999 ★

28	**29**	**30**	**1**	**2** Disney On Ice "75th Anniversary Show"	**3** Disney On Ice "75th Anniversary Show"	**4** Disney On Ice "75th Anniversary Show"
5 Disney On Ice "75th Anniversary Show"	**6**	**7** Pacers 83 vs. San Antonio Spurs 77	**8** Neil Diamond Concert (In The Round)	**9** Kid Rock w/ Powerman 5000 Concert	**10** Pacers 136 vs. Cleveland Cavaliers 88	**11** Pacers 108 vs. Los Angeles Clippers 88
12	**13**	**14** Billy Joel Concert	**15** Pacers 102 vs. Chicago Bulls 91	**16**	**17** Pacers 89 vs. Utah Jazz 74	**18** Purdue Blockbuster Classic Purdue Women vs. Kentucky Purdue Men vs. Ball State
19	**20**	**21** Pacers 113 vs. Seattle SuperSonics 103	**22** Marsh High School Holiday B-Ball Classic Ben Davis vs.Cathedral (Women) LaPorte vs. Chesterton (Men) Muncie Central vs. Jeffersonville (Men)	**23**	**24**	**25** Pacers 101 vs. New York Knicks 90
26	**27** Hoosier Basketball Classic Indiana vs. Canisius Holy Cross vs. UAB	**28** Hoosier Basketball Classic UAB vs. Canisius Indiana vs. Holy Cross	**29** Harlem Globetrotters	**30** Pacers 109 vs. Charlotte Hornets 99	**31** John Mellencamp Millennium Concert	**1**

January 2000

26	27	28	29	30	31	1
2	3	4 Pacers 116 vs. New Jersey Nets 111	5	6	7 Circle City Grand National Rodeo	8 Circle City Grand National Rodeo
9 Circle City Grand National Rodeo	10	11	12 Pacers 117 vs. Washington Wizards 102	13	14 Pacers 111 vs. Los Angeles Lakers 102	15 Ice 6 vs. Topeka ScareCrows 2
16	17	18	19 Pacers 106 vs. Milwaukee Bucks 84	20	21	22 Ice 4 vs. San Antonio Iguanas 1
23/30	24/31	25 Pacers 93 vs. Phoenix Suns 87	26	27 Michael Flatley's Lord of the Dance	28	29 Pacers 94 vs. Miami Heat 84

February 2000

30	31	1 Pacers 99 vs. Boston Celtics 96	2	3	4 Pacers 104 vs. Sacramento Kings 94	5 Ice 5 vs. San Antonio Iguanas 4, shootout
6 Target Stars On Ice Show	7 Pacers 109 vs. Philadelphia 76ers 84	8	9	10	11 Alan Jackson/ Lonestar Concert	12 Ice 8 vs. Memphis RiverKings 3
13	14	15	16 Pacers 109 vs. Toronto Raptors 101	17	18 IHSAA State Wrestling Finals	19 IHSAA State Wrestling Finals
20 Pavarotti Concert	21 Pacers 94 vs. Dallas Mavericks 93	22	23	24 Pacers 100 vs. Chicago Bulls 83	25 Ice 2 vs. Topeka ScareCrows 5	26 Pacers 104 vs. Golden State Warriors 88
27 Ice 6 vs. Huntsville Channel Cats 0	28	29 Pacers 115 vs. Detroit Pistons 105	1	2	3	4

March 2000

27	28	29	1	2	3	4
				Big 10 Conference Women's B-Ball Tournament	**Big 10 Conference Women's B-Ball Tournament**	**Big 10 Conference Women's B-Ball Tournament**
5 Big 10 Conference Women's B-Ball Tournament	**6**	**7** Pacers 90 vs. Denver Nuggets 89	**8** WWF (Rescheduled from January 28)	**9**	**10** Backstreet Boys Concert	**11** Backstreet Boys Concert
12 Pacers 96 vs. Miami Heat 105	**13**	**14**	**15** Ruff Ryders/ Cash Money Concert Featured: DMX, Eve, The Lox, Juvenile, Lil Wayne, The Hot Boyz	**16**	**17** Pacers 111 vs. Houston Rockets 102	**18** Pacers 113 vs. Charlotte Hornets 99
19 Korn Concert	**20**	**21**	**22** Creed Concert	**23** Pacers 84 vs. Milwaukee Bucks 105	**24** Crosby, Stills, Nash & Young Concert	**25** IHSAA Boys Basketball State Championship Class A – Lafayette Central Catholic vs Union (Dugger) Class 2A – Westview vs. Winchester Class 3A – Andrean vs. Brebeuf Class 4A – Marion vs. Bloomington North
26 Pacers 101 vs. Philadelphia 76ers 111	**27**	**28** Boston Pops Concert	**29**	**30** Intersport Slam Dunk Contest In conjunction with NCAA Final 4 – Slam Dunk/3-Pt Shootout	**31** Pacers 109 vs. Minnesota Timberwolves 85	**1**

April 2000

26	27	28	29	30	31	1
						1 NABC All-Star Game College All-Stars vs. Harlem Globetrotters
2 NIKE Hoop Summit High School All-Stars vs. International Team	**3**	**4**	**5** Pacers 105 vs. New Jersey Nets 101	**6**	**7** Pacers 95 vs. Cleveland Cavaliers 94	**8**
9	**10**	**11**	**12** Pacers 77 vs. Toronto Raptors 73	**13**	**14**	**15** Elton John Concert
16	**17**	**18** Champions On Ice Show	**19** Pacers 111 vs. Atlanta Hawks 92	**20** Nine Inch Nails Concert	**21**	**22**
23/30 (23) Pacers 88 vs. Milwaukee Bucks 85 NBA Playoffs 2000, Game 1 of First Round	**24**	**25**	**26**	**27** Pacers 91 vs. Milwaukee Bucks 104 NBA Playoffs 2000, Game 2 of First Round	**28**	**29**

May 2000

30	**1**	**2**	**3**	**4** Pacers 96 vs. Milwaukee Bucks 95 NBA Playoffs 2000, Game 5 of First Round	**5** Gaither Homecoming	**6** Pacers 108 vs. Philadelphia 76ers 91 NBA Playoffs 2000, Game 1 of Conference Semifinals
7	**8** Pacers 103 vs. Philadelphia 76ers 97 NBA Playoffs 2000, Game 2 of Conference Semifinals	**9** Richard Hall Workout in Entry Pavilion	**10** Roy Jones Workout in Entry Pavilion	**11** Boxing Press Conference in Entry Pavilion	**12** Boxing Weigh In	**13** Roy Jones, Jr. Boxing (Eight bouts – Four Title Fights)
14	**15** Pacers 86 vs. Philadelphia 76ers 107 NBA Playoffs 2000, Game 5 of Conference Semifinals	**16**	**17**	**18** Fever 68 vs. Sacramento Monarchs 74 (Preseason)	**19**	**20**
21	**22** WWF Raw	**23** Pacers 102 vs. New York Knicks 88 NBA Playoffs 2000, Game 1 of Conference Finals	**24** Warren Central High School Graduation	**25** Pacers 88 vs. New York Knicks 84 NBA Playoffs 2000, Game 2 of Conference Finals	**26** Tina Turner w/ Lionel Richie Concert	**27**
28	**29**	**30**	**31** Pacers 88 vs. New York Knicks 79 NBA Playoffs 2000, Game 5 of Conference Finals	**1**	**2**	**3**

June 2000

28	**29**	**30**	**31**	**1**	**2**	**3** Fever 82 vs. Orlando Miracle 88 First Regular Season Home Game
4	**5** Fever 80 vs. Miami Sol 59	**6**	**7** North Central High School Graduation	**8**	**9**	**10** Fever 62 vs. New York Liberty 70
11 Pacers 100 vs. Los Angeles Lakers 91 NBA Playoffs 2000, Game 3 of Finals	**12** Fever 70 vs Cleveland Rockers 83	**13**	**14** Pacers 118 vs. Los Angeles Lakers 120 OT NBA Playoffs 2000, Game 4 of Finals	**15**	**16** Pacers 120 vs. Los Angeles Lakers 87 NBA Playoffs 2000, Game 5 of Finals	**17**
18	**19**	**20**	**21** Fever 58 vs. Sacramento Monarchs 70	**22**	**23** Fever 60 vs. New York Liberty 69	**24** Indiana/Kentucky All-Star Basketball Game Girls/Boys Games
25	**26**	**27**	**28** Fever 73 vs. Los Angeles Sparks 82	**29**	**30** Dr. Dre "Up In Smoke" Concert Featuring: Dr. Dre, Snoop Dogg, Warren G	**1**

July 2000

27	28	27	28	29	30	**1** Fever 52 vs. Miami Sol 54
2	**3** Fever 64 vs. Portland Fire 68	**4**	**5** Ricky Martin Concert	**6**	**7**	**8** Fever 65 vs. Phoenix Mercury 66
9	**10**	**11**	**12**	**13**	**14** Fever 62 vs. Seattle Storm 45	**15** Indiana Black Expo Music Heritage Festival Featuring: Earth, Wind & Fire, Teena Marie
16 Indiana Black Expo Music Heritage Festival Featuring: Gerald Levert, Frankie Beverley & Maze, K-Ci & JoJo	**17**	**18**	**19**	**20**	**21**	**22** Fever 80 vs. Charlotte Sting 59
23/30 (30) WCW	**24/31**	**25**	**26**	**27**	**28**	**29** Heritage Keepers

August 2000

30	31	**1**	**2**	**3** Fever 71 vs. Washington Mystics 75	**4** Fever 87 vs. Cleveland Rockers 75	**5**
6	**7** Fever 63 vs. Detroit Shock 74	**8**	**9** Fever 67 vs. Charlotte Sting 51	**10**	**11**	**12**
13	**14**	**15**	**16**	**17**	**18**	**19**
20	**21**	**22**	**23**	**24**	**25**	**26**
27 AC/DC Concert	**28**	**29**	**30**	**31**	1	2

★ September 2000 ★

27	28	29	30	31	1	2
3	4	5	6	7	8	9 **Kiss Concert** w/ Special Guests: Ted Nugent & Skid Row
10	11	12	13	14	15	16
17	18	19	20	21	22 **Tim McGraw & Faith Hill Concert**	23
24	25	26	27 **Ringling Bros. and Barnum & Bailey Circus**	28 **Ringling Bros. and Barnum & Bailey Circus**	29 **Ringling Bros. and Barnum & Bailey Circus**	30 **Ringling Bros. and Barnum & Bailey Circus**

★ October 2000 ★

1 **Ringling Bros. and Barnum & Bailey Circus**	2	3	4	5	6	7
8	9	10	11 **Pacers vs. Minnesota Timberwolves** (Preseason Game)	12 **Pacers vs. Denver Nuggets** (Preseason Game)	13	14
15 **Pacers vs. Sacramento Kings** (Preseason Game)	16	17	18	19	20 **Pacers vs. Los Angeles Clippers** (Preseason Game)	21
22 **Dixie Chicks Concert**	23	24 **Blackwatch**	25 **'N Sync Concert**	26 **'N Sync Concert**	27	28
29	30	31	1	2	3	4

Blue & Gold Ball

Grand Opening

The Ribbon Cutting

Bob Costas served as the Master of Ceremonies as city and state dignitaries helped to cut the ribbon and open Conseco Fieldhouse on Saturday, November 6, 1999. Shortly after the ribbon cutting, confetti flooded the west plaza on Pennsylvania Street and 18,345 fans caught their breathtaking first views of the Fieldhouse.

Pacers Fan Fest

The Pacers Fan Fest, presented by **Conseco**, is expected to remain one of the largest one-day events in the history of the building. This four-hour open house featured live bands, clowns, games and tours. More than 75,000 people toured the building during the event.

The 50 Greatest Players

(Left to Right) Indiana natives, Oscar Robertson, John Wooden and Larry Bird, were part of Indiana's 50 Greatest Players honored during halftime of the Indiana Pacers' opening game on November 6.

50 Greatest Players

Presented by Logo Athletic

STEVE ALFORD

DAMON BAILEY

WALT BELLAMY

KENT BENSON

LARRY BIRD

RON BONHAM

ROGER BROWN

HALLIE BRYANT

QUINN BUCKNER

DON BUSE

AUSTIN CARR

LOUIE DAMPIER

MEL DANIELS

ADRIAN DANTLEY

TERRY DISCHINGER

WILLIE GARDNER

BILL GARRETT

ALAN HENDERSON

BILLY KELLER

SHAWN KEMP

BILLY KNIGHT

BOB LEONARD

CLYDE LOVELLETTE

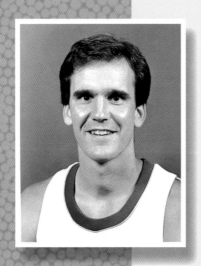

KYLE MACY

GEORGE McGINNIS

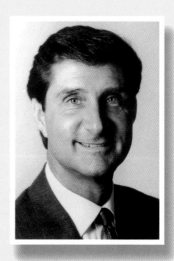

JOHN McGLOCKLIN

WILLIE MERRIWEATHER

REGGIE MILLER

RICK MOUNT

CHARLES MURPHY

BOBBY PLUMP

LATAUNYA POLLARD

JIMMY RAYL

OSCAR ROBERTSON

GLENN ROBINSON

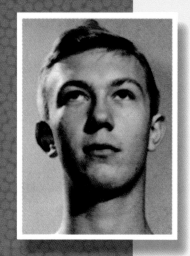

DON SCHLUNDT

DAVE SCHELLHASE

BILLY SHEPHERD

SCOTT SKILES

JERRY SLOAN

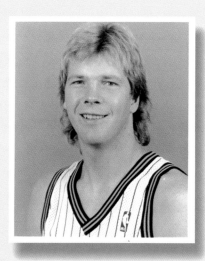

RIK SMITS

HOMER STONEBRAKER

ISIAH THOMAS

DICK VAN ARSDALE

TOM VAN ARSDALE

FUZZY VANDIVIER

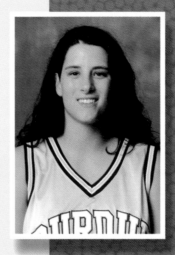

STEPHANIE McCARTY

JOHNNY WILSON

RANDY WITTMAN

JOHN WOODEN

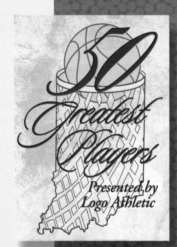

Indiana Pacers
Season Recap

On November 6, 1999 the Indiana Pacers christened their new home in a very special way. In a moving halftime ceremony, the 50 Greatest Players in the state's illustrious basketball history were honored before the adoring eyes of a sellout Conseco Fieldhouse crowd, on the opening night of the regular season.

The night was a hit for everyone, as the Pacers broke in their $183 million state-of-the-art building with a 115-108 win against the Boston Celtics.

And from there, things only got better.

Seven months after that glorious evening, the Pacers thrilled the city and electrified an entire basketball-crazed state by reaching the NBA Finals for the first time in franchise history.

Vitaly Potapenko of the Boston Celtics scored the first basket at Conseco Fieldhouse.

Although they fell just short of winning the championship, the Pacers proved once and for all to themselves and to their fans that they indeed possess championship mettle.

"We're deep," said star guard Reggie Miller, who made the NBA All-Star team for a Pacers team-record fifth time. "We play well together. We're well coached. We're well disciplined.

"Hopefully, with all those characteristics, good things will lay at the end of the rainbow for us."

Pacers Facts

Between November 25, 1999 and March 12, 2000, the Pacers went on a 25 consecutive home game winning streak.

To the delight of their fans, the Pacers nearly claimed the pot of gold at the end of last season's rainbow.

After winning their third Central Division title and their first-ever Eastern Conference championship, the Pacers took on the formidable challenge of squaring off for the NBA title against the Los Angeles Lakers and their massive All-Star center, 7-foot-1, 330-pound Shaquille O'Neal.

Although the Lakers, who finished with the best regular season record in the NBA, won the championship, they didn't do so until being pushed to the limit by the Pacers — a team most media pundits wrote off as past their prime in their preseason analysis and predictions.

Owners of home court advantage throughout the playoffs, the Lakers won the best-of seven Finals series 4-2. But that belies what was actually a much closer series.

With the exception of a convincing 104-87 Game 1 win by the Lakers, the other five contests were tightly wound — except for Game 5, which the Pacers won in a spectacular 120-87 blowout.

The stunning win not only narrowed L.A.'s series advantage to 3-2, but also ensured that the tradition-rich Lakers — who would host Game 6 and, if necessary, Game 7 — did not celebrate winning a championship on the Conseco Fieldhouse floor.

It also gave fans a chance to see the Pacers win their last home game of the season.

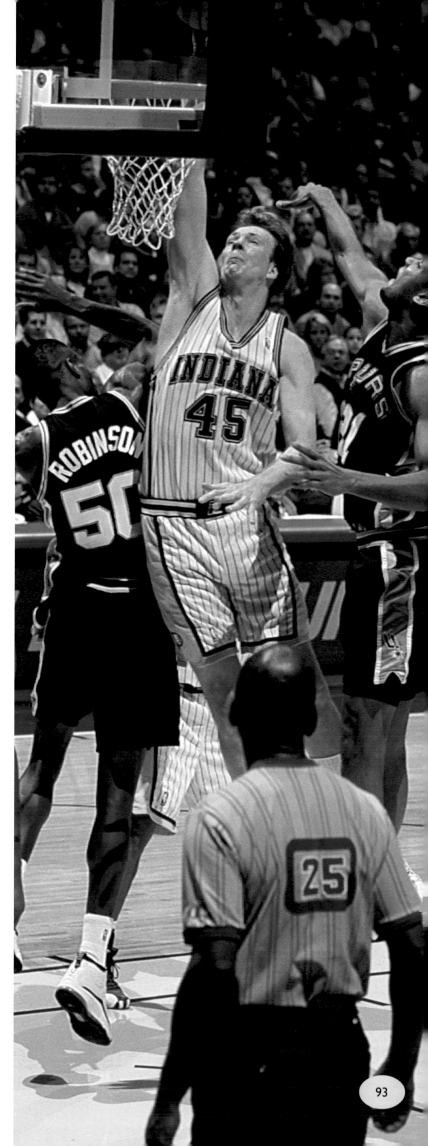

"It was a great win," said forward Jalen Rose, who topped all Pacers' scorers with 32 points in Game 5. "We talked about it being do-or-die. I talked about us not allowing them to celebrate on our home floor. I was serious about that. That would be a bad feeling to end our season on."

"The way our crowd has watched us play and perform all year, they're excited about this moment. This is the first time the Pacers have been to the NBA Finals. It can be old hat in California. They've had great players, great teams, their city thrives on so many things. Indiana thrives on basketball.

"For this to be happening for our town," Rose continued, "we didn't want them to leave the game feeling like the season was a disappointment."

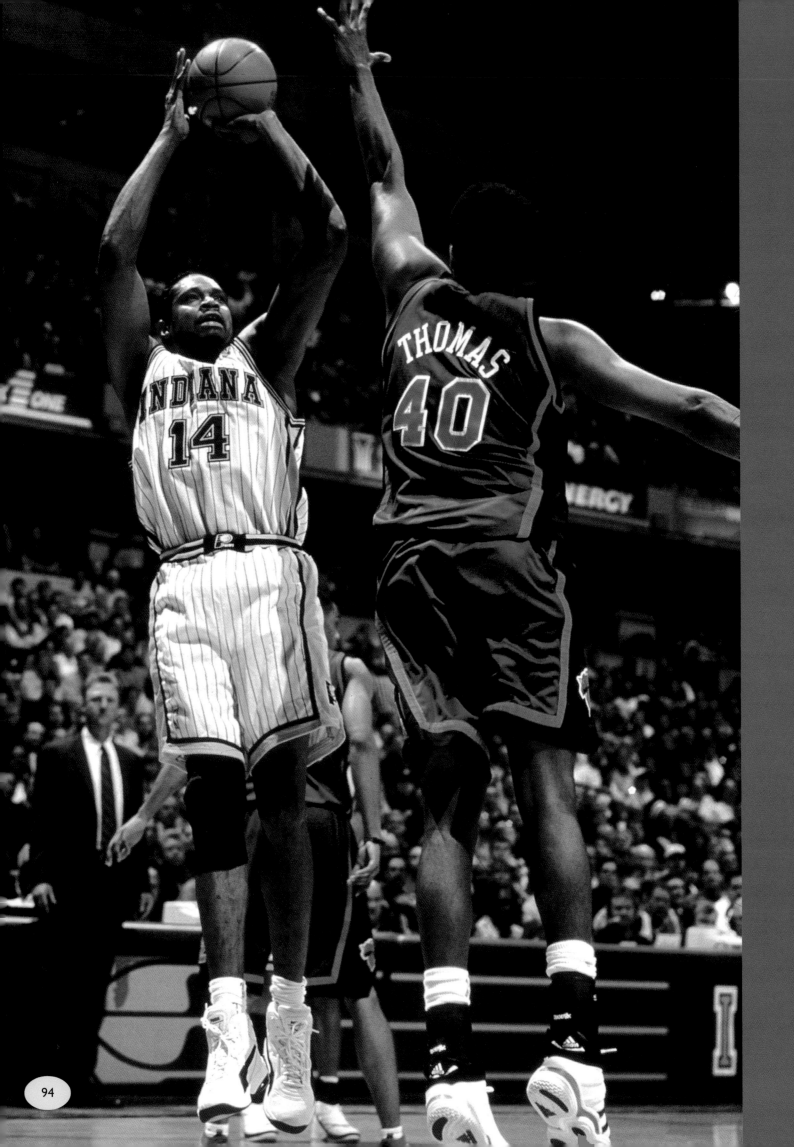

The Pacers lost only five home games during their regular season at Conseco Fieldhouse. Finishing 36-5 at home, the Pacers only losses were to Atlanta, Detroit, Miami, Milwaukee and Philadelphia.

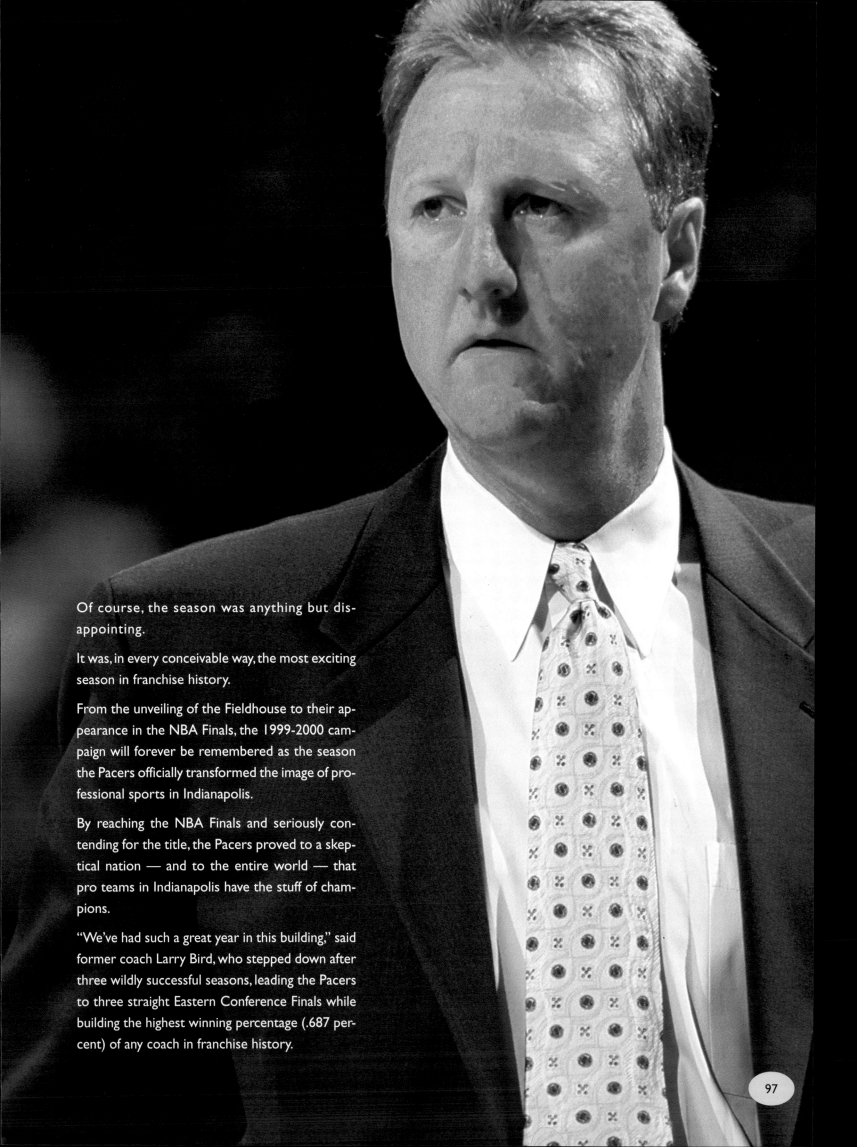

Of course, the season was anything but disappointing.

It was, in every conceivable way, the most exciting season in franchise history.

From the unveiling of the Fieldhouse to their appearance in the NBA Finals, the 1999-2000 campaign will forever be remembered as the season the Pacers officially transformed the image of professional sports in Indianapolis.

By reaching the NBA Finals and seriously contending for the title, the Pacers proved to a skeptical nation — and to the entire world — that pro teams in Indianapolis have the stuff of champions.

"We've had such a great year in this building," said former coach Larry Bird, who stepped down after three wildly successful seasons, leading the Pacers to three straight Eastern Conference Finals while building the highest winning percentage (.687 percent) of any coach in franchise history.

1999-2000 Pacers Season Stats

NOVEMBER

Day	Date		Opponent		Result	O'all	Home	Road	Attendance	Scoring Leader	Rebound Leader	Assists Leader
Tue.	2	at	New Jersey	W	119-112	1-0	0-0	1-0	13,051	Miller 27	Davis 13	Jackson 5
Thu.	4	at	Charlotte	L	89-98	1-1	0-0	1-1	15,762	Miller 20	Davis/Rose 7	Jackson 7
Sat.	6		Boston	W	115-108	2-1	1-0	1-1	*18,345	Miller 29	Davis 11	Jackson 8
Tue.	9	at	Miami	L	101-113	2-2	1-0	1-2	15,200	Rose 17	Davis 10	Jackson 4
Thu.	11		Orlando	W	116-101	3-2	2-0	1-2	*18,345	Miller 21	Rose 8	Rose 7
Sat.	13		Washington	W	105-83	4-2	3-0	1-2	*18,345	Rose 16	Davis 8	Best/Jackson 6
Mon.	15	at	Houston	W	96-87	5-2	3-0	2-2	14,866	Harrington 18	Davis 11	Jackson 7
Tue.	16		San Antonio	L	87-90 OT	5-3	3-0	2-3	15,905	Rose 28	Davis 10	Jackson/Miller/Perkins 4
Fri.	19		Atlanta	L	99-105	5-4	3-1	2-3	*18,345	Miller/Smits 21	Harrington 8	Jackson 12
Sat.	20	at	Cleveland	W	107-98	6-4	3-1	3-3	13,806	Rose 22	Croshere 8	Jackson/Rose 9
Mon.	22	at	Boston	L	85-95	6-5	3-1	3-4	15,728	Davis 19	Davis 12	Jackson 8
Thu.	25		Detroit	L	99-107	6-6	3-2	3-4	*18,345	Smits 23	Davis 8	Jackson 10
Fri.	26		Vancouver	W	105-86	7-6	4-2	3-4	*18,345	Smits 17	Croshere/Smits 5	Best 6
Sun.	28	at	Seattle	L	91-102	7-7	4-2	3-5	14,644	Davis 19	Davis 15	Best 5
Mon.	29	at	Portland	W	93-91	8-7	4-2	4-5	20,049	Rose 22	Davis 12	Jackson 9

DECEMBER

Day	Date		Opponent		Result	O'all	Home	Road	Attendance	Scoring Leader	Rebound Leader	Assists Leader
Wed.	1	at	Vancouver	W	96-89	9-7	4-2	5-5	11,683	Miller 26	Croshere 9	Jackson 10
Fri.	3	at	Utah	W	100-75	10-7	4-2	6-5	19,084	Miller 31	Davis 13	Jackson 9
Tue.	7		San Antonio	W	83-77	11-7	5-2	6-5	*18,345	Miller 23	Davis 16	Jackson 9
Fri.	10		Cleveland	W	136-88	12-7	6-2	6-5	*18,345	Smits 25	Davis 20	Miller 8
Sat.	11		LA Clippers	W	108-90	13-7	7-2	6-5	*18,345	Miller 26	Davis 18	Jackson 9
Tue.	14	at	Toronto	L	97-105	13-8	7-2	6-6	15,774	Rose 21	Davis 10	Best 7
Wed.	15		Chicago	W	102-91	14-8	8-2	6-6	*18,345	Croshere 21	Smits 8	Jackson 5
Fri.	17		Utah	W	89-74	15-8	9-2	6-6	*18,345	Miller 19	Croshere 11	Jackson 6
Sat.	18	at	Milwaukee	L	95-109	15-9	9-2	6-7	15,236	Miller 21	Davis 15	Jackson 10
Tue.	21		Seattle	W	113-103	16-9	10-2	6-7	*18,345	Miller 31	Davis 9	Jackson/Rose 11
Sat.	25		New York	W	101-90	17-9	11-2	6-7	*18,345	Miller 26	Croshere 10	Jackson 7
Mon.	27	at	Chicago	W	103-91	18-9	11-2	7-7	22,169	Davis 21	Davis 8	Jackson 10
Wed.	29	at	Atlanta	W	116-89	19-9	11-2	8-7	16,117	Miller 25	Davis 12	Jackson 14
Thu.	30		Charlotte	W	109-99	20-9	12-2	8-7	*18,345	Miller 30	Davis 11	Jackson 11

JANUARY

Day	Date		Opponent		Result	O'all	Home	Road	Attendance	Scoring Leader	Rebound Leader	Assists Leader
Tue.	4		New Jersey	W	116-111	21-9	13-2	8-7	*18,345	Miller 24	Smits 9	Jackson 15
Thu.	6	at	Denver	W	102-87	22-9	13-2	9-7	14,569	Miller 20	Croshere/Davis/Perkins 7	Jackson 10
Sat.	8	at	LA Clippers	L	94-107	22-10	13-2	9-8	17,004	Best 20	Davis/Rose/Smits 6	Jackson 6
Sun.	9	at	Sacramento	L	113-116	22-11	13-2	9-9	17,317	Croshere 22	Davis 12	Best 8
Wed.	12		Washington	W	117-102	23-11	14-2	9-9	*18,345	Rose 25	Davis 13	Jackson 13
Fri.	14		LA Lakers	W	111-102	24-11	15-2	9-9	*18,345	Miller 22	Croshere 12	Jackson 8
Sat.	15	at	Orlando	W	96-89	25-11	15-2	10-9	14,456	Croshere 14	Davis 11	Rose 6
Mon.	17	at	Minnesota	L	100-101	25-12	15-2	10-10	16,731	Smits 20	Croshere 13	Jackson 11
Wed.	19		Milwaukee	W	106-84	26-12	16-2	10-10	*18,345	Miller 29	Davis 13	Jackson 13
Fri.	21	at	Washington	L	113-123	26-13	16-2	10-11	17,055	Miller/Rose 21	Davis 9	Jackson 13
Sat.	22	at	Philadelphia	L	97-103	26-14	16-2	10-12	20,623	Miller 28	Davis 15	Jackson 9
Mon.	24	at	Chicago	L	82-83	26-15	16-2	10-13	21,911	Rose 18	Davis 11	Jackson 12
Tue.	25		Phoenix	W	93-87	27-15	17-2	10-13	*18,345	Miller 21	Davis/Rose 9	Jackson 8
Sat.	29		Miami	W	94-84	28-15	18-2	10-13	*18,345	Miller 30	Croshere/Davis 6	Jackson 8

FEBRUARY

Day	Date		Opponent		Result	O'all	Home	Road	Attendance	Scoring Leader	Rebound Leader	Assists Leader
Tue.	1		Boston	W	99-96	29-15	19-2	10-13	*18,345	Smits 26	Davis 14	Jackson 7
Fri.	4		Sacramento	W	104-94	30-15	20-2	10-13	*18,345	Rose 22	Davis 13	Jackson 15
Sat.	5	at	Orlando	L	102-107	30-16	20-2	10-14	15,421	Rose 25	Davis 14	Best/Jackson/Rose 4
Mon.	7		Philadelphia	W	109-84	31-16	21-2	10-14	*18,345	Miller 32	Rose 7	McKey/Rose 6
Wed.	9	at	Boston	W	113-104	32-16	21-2	11-14	18,328	Rose 23	Davis 11	Jackson 9
Wed.	16		Toronto	W	109-101	33-16	22-2	11-14	*18,345	Rose 32	Davis 13	Jackson 15
Thu.	17	at	Milwaukee	W	92-90	34-16	22-2	12-14	14,376	Miller 23	Croshere/Davis/Jackson 9	Jackson 9
Sat.	19	at	New York	L	73-87	34-17	22-2	12-15	19,763	Miller 16	Davis 16	Jackson 6
Mon.	21		Dallas	W	94-93	35-17	23-2	12-15	*18,345	Rose 28	Davis/McKey 8	Jackson 6
Wed.	23	at	Detroit	W	118-111	36-17	23-2	13-15	16,371	Smits 29	Smits 9	Jackson 14
Thu.	24		Chicago	W	100-83	37-17	24-2	13-15	*18,345	Rose 22	McKey 10	Jackson 7
Sat.	26		Golden State	W	104-88	38-17	25-2	13-15	*18,345	Rose 29	Perkins 7	Jackson 9
Tue.	29		Detroit	W	115-105	39-17	26-2	13-15	*18,345	Miller 24	Smits 12	Jackson 13

MARCH

Day	Date		Opponent	W/L	Result	O'all	Home	Road	Attendance	Scoring Leader	Rebound Leader	Assists Leader
Thu.	2	at	Phoenix	L	87-118	39-18	26-2	13-16	19,023	Best 20	Croshere/Davis 9	Jackson 8
Fri.	3	at	LA Lakers	L	92-107	39-19	26-2	13-17	18,997	Miller 22	Davis 13	Jackson 6
Sun.	5	at	Golden State	W	114-95	40-19	26-2	14-17	15,283	Croshere 18	Davis 8	Jackson 8
Tue.	7		Denver	W	90-89	41-19	27-2	14-17	*18,345	Rose 19	Davis 11	Rose 9
Thu.	9		Portland	W	127-119 OT	42-19	28-2	14-17	*18,345	Jackson 23	Davis 13	Jackson 9
Fri.	10	at	Cleveland	W	95-92	43-19	28-2	15-17	20,562	Miller 28	McKey/Smits 8	Jackson 7
Sun.	12		Miami	L	96-105	43-20	28-3	15-17	*18,345	Miller 26	Davis 8	Jackson 7
Tue.	14	at	Dallas	L	90-111	43-21	28-3	15-18	15,761	Best 26	Croshere/Rose 13	Best 5
Wed.	15	at	Atlanta	W	113-107	44-21	28-3	16-18	14,454	Rose 32	Croshere 11	Jackson 10
Fri.	17		Houston	W	111-102	45-21	29-3	16-18	*18,345	Rose 35	Croshere 13	Jackson 8
Sat.	18		Charlotte	W	113-99	46-21	30-3	16-18	*18,345	Rose 22	Croshere 11	Jackson 9
Tue.	21		New York	W	95-91	47-21	31-3	16-18	*18,345	Rose 28	Croshere 8	Jackson 7
Thu.	23		Milwaukee	L	84-105	47-22	31-4	16-18	*18,345	Rose 22	Croshere 7	Jackson 5
Sun.	26		Philadelphia	L	101-111	47-23	31-5	16-18	*18,345	Rose 19	Smits 7	Best/Jackson 5
Tue.	28	at	New Jersey	L	111-106	47-24	31-5	16-19	17,676	Rose 27	Croshere 10	Jackson 11
Fri.	31		Minnesota	W	109-85	48-24	32-5	16-19	*18,345	Best 27	Davis 9	Best 7

APRIL

Day	Date		Opponent	W/L	Result	O'all	Home	Road	Attendance	Scoring Leader	Rebound Leader	Assists Leader
Sun.	2	at	Toronto	W	104-83	49-24	32-5	17-19	19,800	Rose 23	Davis/Perkins 7	Jackson 10
Wed.	5		New Jersey	W	105-101	50-24	33-5	17-19	*18,345	Smits 25	Davis 11	Jackson 8
Fri.	7		Cleveland	W	95-94	51-24	34-5	17-19	*18,345	Rose 26	Rose 13	Jackson 6
Sun.	9	at	Charlotte	L	80-96	51-25	34-5	17-20	19,312	Rose 18	Davis 14	Jackson 8
Mon.	10	at	New York	L	81-83	51-26	34-5	17-21	19,763	Jackson 13	Davis 12	Jackson 5
Wed.	12		Toronto	W	77-73	52-26	35-5	17-21	*18,345	Rose 24	Davis 14	Jackson/Rose 4
Fri.	14	at	Miami	W	105-101	53-26	35-5	18-21	19,821	Miller 26	Davis 7	Jackson 5
Sun.	16	at	Detroit	W	112-101	54-26	35-5	19-21	17,629	Miller 21	Davis 15	Jackson 9
Mon.	17	at	Philadelphia	W	92-90	55-26	35-5	20-21	20,797	Mullin 21	Smits 10	Rose 9
Wed.	19		Atlanta	W	111-92	56-26	36-5	20-21	*18,345	Rose 19	Foster 13	Jackson 8

PLAYOFFS
FIRST ROUND

Day	Date		Opponent	W/L	Result	O'all	Home	Road	Attendance	Scoring Leader	Rebound Leader	Assists Leader
Sun.	23		Milwaukee	W	88-85	1-0	1-0	0-0	*18,345	Rose 26	Davis 17	Jackson 11
Thu.	27		Milwaukee	L	91-104	1-1	1-1	0-0	*18,345	Croshere 16	Davis 12	Jackson 5
Sat.	29	at	Milwaukee	W	96-109	2-1	1-1	1-0	18,717	Miller 34	Croshere 11	Miller/Rose 5

MAY

Day	Date		Opponent	W/L	Result	O'all	Home	Road	Attendance	Scoring Leader	Rebound Leader	Assists Leader
Mon.	1	at	Milwaukee	L	87-100	2-2	1-1	1-1	18,072	Rose 17	Davis 10	Jackson 6
Thu.	4		Milwaukee	W	96-95	3-2	2-1	1-1	*18,345	Miller 41	Davis 12	Jackson 8

EASTERN CONFERENCE SEMIFINALS

Day	Date		Opponent	W/L	Result	O'all	Home	Road	Attendance	Scoring Leader	Rebound Leader	Assists Leader
Sat.	6		Philadelphia	W	108-91	4-2	3-1	1-1	*18,345	Miller/Rose 40	Croshere 11	Jackson 10
Mon.	8		Philadelphia	W	103-97	5-2	4-1	1-1	*18,345	Rose 30	Rose 7	Jackson 14
Wed.	10	at	Philadelphia	W	97-89	6-2	4-1	2-1	20,823	Miller 29	Davis 17	Jackson 8
Sat.	13	at	Philadelphia	L	90-92	6-3	4-1	2-2	20,675	Smits 20	Davis 11	Jackson 7
Mon.	15		Philadelphia	L	86-107	6-4	4-2	2-2	*18,345	Smits 15	Davis 8	Jackson/Rose 6
Fri.	19	at	Philadelphia	W	106-90	7-4	4-2	3-2	20,969	Miller 25	Davis 11	Jackson 11

EASTERN CONFERENCE FINALS

Day	Date		Opponent	W/L	Result	O'all	Home	Road	Attendance	Scoring Leader	Rebound Leader	Assists Leader
Tue.	23		New York	W	102-88	8-4	5-2	3-2	*18,345	Croshere 22	Davis 16	Jackson 13
Thu.	25		New York	W	88-84	9-4	6-2	3-2	*18,345	Rose 24	Davis 16	Jackson 5
Sat.	27		New York	L	95-98	9-5	6-2	3-3	19,763	Rose 26	Davis 16	Jackson/Rose 6
Mon.	29	at	New York	L	89-91	9-6	6-2	3-4	19,763	Miller 24	Davis 11	Jackson 7
Wed.	31		New York	W	88-79	10-6	7-2	3-4	*18,345	Best 24	McKey 9	Jackson 7

JUNE

Day	Date		Opponent	W/L	Result	O'all	Home	Road	Attendance	Scoring Leader	Rebound Leader	Assists Leader
Fri.	2	at	New York	W	93-80	11-6	7-2	4-4	19,763	Miller 34	Davis 16	Best/Jackson 4

NBA FINALS

Day	Date		Opponent	W/L	Result	O'all	Home	Road	Attendance	Scoring Leader	Rebound Leader	Assists Leader
Wed.	7	at	L.A. Lakers	L	87-104	11-7	7-2	4-5	18,997	Jackson 18	Davis 8	Jackson 7
Fri.	9	at	L.A. Lakers	L	104-111	11-8	7-2	4-6	18,997	Rose 30	Davis 10	Jackson 8
Sun.	11		Indiana	W	100-91	12-8	8-2	4-6	*18,345	Miller 33	Davis 12	Jackson 2
Wed.	14		Indiana	L	118-120 OT	12-9	8-3	4-6	*18,345	Miller 35	Davis 8	Jackson 7
Fri.	16		Indiana	W	120-87	13-9	9-3	4-6	*18,345	Rose 32	Croshere 9	Jackson 7
Mon.	19	at	L.A. Lakers	L	111-116	13-10	9-3	4-7	18,997	Rose 29	Davis 14	Jackson 11

* denotes home sellout

"Our fans have supported us," said Bird, whose career regular-season record is 147-67. "We've had great success in here."

Indeed they have.

In addition to winning the Eastern Conference and reaching the NBA Finals for the first time, the Pacers — also for the first time — sold out their entire home schedule. They finished with a 56-26 regular-season record — the second-best in franchise history and the best in the Eastern Conference — and tied the Lakers for the NBA's best home record at 36-5.

On top of those achievements, the Pacers boasted a pair of All-Stars in Miller and veteran forward Dale Davis, who made his All-Star debut.

"Like I said, we've had such a great year here," Bird said after the Pacers' dramatic Game 5 win in the Finals. "We struggled at times at Market Square Arena, but here we played extremely well this year. I think it's important for us to come out and play well because the support has been there all year long.

"We've been sold out every game, so I think it's important for us to come out and assure our fans we're not going to quit and try to take this thing as far as we can."

Although the Pacers had different heroes rise to the occasion on different nights, it is indisputable they went as far as they did because of the season-long one-two punch of Miller and Rose.

101

No stranger to performing playoff magic, Miller — who has spent all 13 of his distinguished NBA seasons with the Pacers — had yet another spectacular postseason. He averaged a team-leading 24 points per game throughout the playoffs and averaged 24 ppg against the Lakers.

His finest hour, however, happened in the first round in a precarious best-of-five series against the Milwaukee Bucks.

His team tottering on the brink of elimination with the series knotted at 2-2, Miller sported a blue "Superman" T-shirt during the pregame warm-up of the decisive Game 5 in the Fieldhouse. He then soared for a career-playoff-high 41 points to lift the Pacers to a thrilling 96-95 win.

Suffice it to say, Miller's Superman-like performance salvaged both the series and Indiana's bid for reaching the Finals.

"I'm enjoying the playoffs," Miller said as he continued his offensive onslaught into the Eastern Conference Semifinals against Philadelphia. "I've got to continue to be aggressive and look for my shot, because when I've got it clicking, then everyone else seems to fall into place.

"It's when I don't shoot, when I'm not aggressive, that's when our offense is somewhat stagnant."

Besides his 41-point explosion against the Bucks, Miller's other playoff highlights included:

• A game-high 34 points in a critical First Round Game 3 win at Milwaukee.

• A 40-point explosion in the Eastern Conference Semifinals win against the Philadelphia 76ers.

• A team-high 33 points in a NBA Finals Game 3 win against Los Angeles.

• A 25-point performance in the NBA Finals Game 5 rout of the Lakers.

"I don't know if you can necessarily feel it coming on," Miller said of his rare ability to conjure playoff miracles. "But I really feel that I have good use of my legs. I'm seeing the rim much better. But what is really carrying me, I'm taking the ball off the dribble a little bit more.

"I know it might look like I'm taking more jumpers, but being able to get to the hole and using my height (6-foot-7) advantage allows me to get good looks."

As for the regular season, Miller averaged 18.1 points and finished second in the league in free throw shooting (91 percent) and was fourth in total 3-point field goals (165).

In conjunction with Rose's breakout season, the Pacers featured an explosive combination that baffled most defenses.

"He (Rose) carried us a lot of games during the regular season this year when my offense had gone south," said Miller, the NBA's all-time leader in three-point baskets. "But when we're both clicking, that's when this team is at its best.

"It's hard to beat us when we're both clicking like that. That's how we've got to do it. We've got to work off one another."

And speaking of Rose, the versatile small forward/point guard proved that he is a star on the rise by putting together what was easily the best season of his six-year career.

After three years of coming off the bench, Rose earned the starting small forward job in training camp and made the most of his opportunity.

The only Pacers player who can score from the perimeter and consistently beat defenders off the dribble, the 6-8 Rose ended Miller's 10-year reign as the team's season scoring champion by averaging 18.2 points during the regular season. But Rose was more than just a scorer.

The first triple-double at Conseco Fieldhouse was accomplished by Mark Jackson on February 4 vs. the Sacramento Kings (15 points, 10 rebounds, 15 assists).

Because of his ability to play in the back court as well as small forward, Rose was an assists producer and a capable rebounder who also evolved into a strong locker room leader.

Not surprisingly, Rose earned the NBA's Most Improved Player Award.

"He's very good with the ball," Bird said. "He can take quick dribbles and pull up (and shoot). He keeps the defense off balance.

"When he's hitting his shots, it's almost impossible to stop him."

Rose came into full bloom for the simple reason that he takes pride in his work.

Reggie Miller and Jalen Rose each scored 40 points in Game One of the Eastern Conference Semifinals against Philadelphia on May 6. This marked the first time in the history of the Pacers that two players had scored 40+ points in the same game (playoffs or regular season).

Jalen Rose is presented with the NBA's "Most Improved Player" Award for the 1999-2000 season. Russ Granik, Deputy Commissioner and Chief Operating Office of the NBA, presents the award.

"Well, I'm a hard guy to please out there, to be honest," said Rose, who, like Miller and fellow teammates Austin Croshere and Sam Perkins, signed a new contract after the season. "I try to be steady. I try to be persistent.

"I pride myself on being a team player and a winner, and I do what I can to help my squad."

Rose's postseason highlights included:

• A career-playoff-high 40 points in the Eastern Conference Semifinals win against Philadelphia.

• 21 points in the 100-91 NBA Finals Game 3 win against the Lakers.

• 14 points and five assists in a heartbreaking 120-118 overtime loss in the NBA Finals Game 4 versus Los Angeles.

• A team-high-tying 25 points in the NBA Finals Game 5 versus the Lakers.

Because of his propensity for big nights, it's little wonder that first-year coach Isiah Thomas — a long-time Rose acquaintance — looks forward to having Rose back in the fold this season.

"I love Jalen Rose as a player," said Thomas, who led Indiana University to the 1981 NCAA Championship. "I've known him since he was in grade school. I had him in camps, and I watched him play in high school and in college and watched him develop as a pro.

"When you look at Jalen, he's an exceptional basketball player, very versatile and capable of playing three positions on the floor."

As invaluable as their services were, Rose and Miller were not the only catalysts behind the Pacers' march to the Finals.

Dale Davis made the All-Star team. Austin Croshere on many nights played like an All-Star. Crafty 38-year-old backup center Sam Perkins often performed like a 28-year-old. Veteran 7-4 center Rik Smits still packed an offensive punch on many nights. Speedy point guard Travis Best routinely provided a defensive spark and clutch shots off the bench. And, steady starting point guard Mark Jackson kept the Pacers' offense running smoothly.

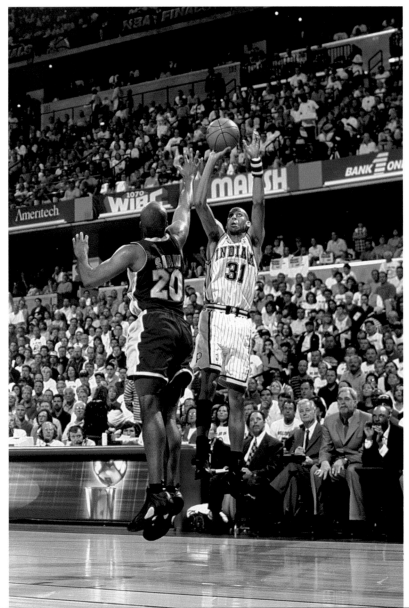

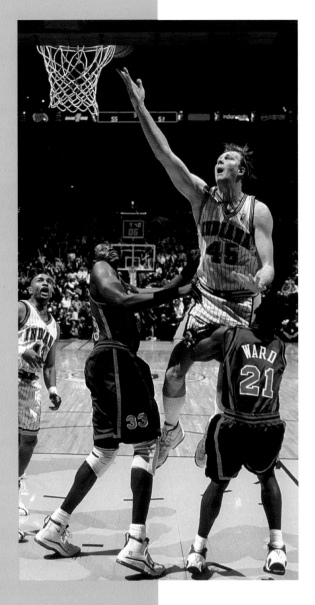

On other nights, backup forwards Derrick McKey, Chris Mullin and Al Harrington provided the impetus for wins. Toward the end of the regular season, rookie forwards Jonathan Bender and Jeff Foster contributed significant minutes to victories.

And every player who returns this season looks forward to finishing what was started last season.

"The opportunity to finish business that we started last year was a huge part of that (decision to re-sign with Indiana)," said Croshere, who averaged 10.3 points and 6.4 rebounds during the regular season. "Being in the Finals last year was the most important thing that I've done as a basketball player.

"The opportunity to get back there far outweighed any of the positives that the other teams could have offered."

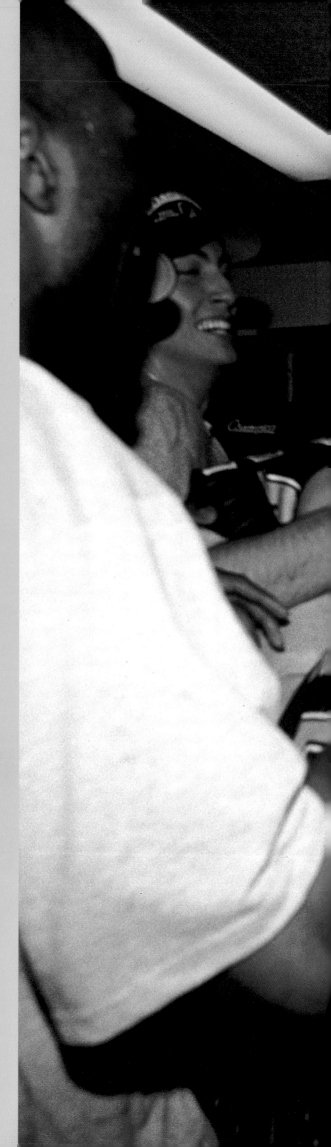

Pacers Facts

The Pacers' best offensive production at Conseco Fieldhouse was 136 points against the Cleveland Cavaliers on December 10. In this game, the Pacers also set a Fieldhouse record by shooting 62 percent from the field.

Rose shares Croshere's sentiment.

"My head and my heart the entire time was to be an Indiana Pacer," Rose said. "I always knew I wanted to be a Pacer, so it was an easy decision for me.

"I said from the beginning that I was going to continue to remain an Indiana Pacer and try to do what I could to help this team and city win a championship."

Rose & Co. will have another chance to accomplish that goal this season.

Indiana Fever
Season Recap

After several months of preparation, the Indiana Fever finally took the Conseco Fieldhouse floor on May 18, 2000 as one of the four new expansion teams in the Women's National Basketball Association (WNBA). Four months later, the Fever finished the season as one of the best teams in the WNBA in attendance. With an average of 11,267 fans per game, the team ranked fourth highest, with only playoff-bound Washington, New York and Houston averaging more fans per game.

INDIANA FEVER SCORES

PRESEASON

May
18   **Sacramento 74, Indiana 68**

REGULAR SEASON (home games in boldface)

June
 1   Indiana 57, Miami 54
 3   **Orlando 88, Indiana 82**
 5   **Indiana 80, Miami 59**
 9   Detroit 80, Indiana 76
 10   **New York 70, Indiana 62**
 12   **Cleveland 83, Indiana 70**
17   Indiana 79, Orlando 54
18   Detroit 111, Indiana 74
 21   **Sacramento 70, Indiana 58**
 23   **New York 69, Indiana 60**
24   Houston 93, Indiana 67
 28   **Los Angeles 82, Indiana 73**
30   New York 72, Indiana 70

July
 1   **Miami 54, Indiana 52**
 3   **Portland 68, Indiana 64**
 6   Orlando 72, Indiana 60
 8   **Phoenix 66, Indiana 65**
12   Indiana 81, Washington 58
 14   **Indiana 64, Seattle 45**
15   Cleveland 79, Indiana 55
20   Washington 85, Indiana 74
 22   **Indiana 80, Charlotte 59**
24   Charlotte 82, Indiana 78 (OT)
26   Phoenix 79, Indiana 65
28   Indiana 73, Portland 58
29   Utah 79, Indiana 71

August
 1   Seattle 66, Indiana 60
 3   **Washington 75, Indiana 71**
 4   **Indiana 87, Cleveland 75**
 6   Minnesota 80, Indiana 75
 7   **Detroit 74, Indiana 63**
 9   **Indiana 67, Charlotte 51**

The Fever's team nickname was announced on December 17, at the Indianapolis Artsgarden at Circle Centre Mall. David Morway, Sr. Vice President/Basketball Administration of Pacers Sports & Entertainment; Donnie Walsh, PS&E's President; Kelly Krauskropf, Chief Operating Officer of the Indiana Fever; Stephanie McCarty, Indiana Fever player; and Anne Donovan, Interim Head Coach of the Indiana Fever display the team's new logo.

In June 1999, the Indiana Pacers were awarded an expansion franchise in the WNBA. Shortly thereafter, the Pacers announced the hiring of Kelly Krauskopf as the team's Chief Operating Officer. Krauskopf was in the forefront of the development of the WNBA after serving as the league's Director of Basketball Operations from 1996-1998.

In August 1999, U.S. Women's National Team head coach Nell Fortner was named the head coach of the new Indiana franchise. However, due to Fortner's commitments to the U.S. Women's Olympic Basketball team, the Fever announced the hiring of Hall-of-Famer Anne Donovan as the team's inaugural season head coach. Donovan will become an assistant coach for the 2001 season after Fortner takes over her coaching duties with the Fever.

On December 15, 1999, the members of the inaugural Indiana Fever team began to fall into place as seven players were acquired in the WNBA's 2000 Expansion Draft. The remainder of the players were acquired through the WNBA's Draft held in April and through the team's local tryouts.

Training camp opened for the Fever on May 3 with 18 players attempting to secure a position on the team. Two weeks later, the Fever played its first preseason game at Conseco Fieldhouse; hosting the Sacramento Monarchs. Indiana lost 74-68 in its home debut, but played the Western Conference power Monarchs tough. The Fever ended its four-game preseason schedule with a 1-3 mark, its one win coming at Orlando on May 26.

The Fever opened the regular season against another 2000 expansion team — the Miami Sol, on June 1. In a nationally televised game on Lifetime TV, the Fever erased a 17-point second-half deficit, took its first lead of the game with just under three minutes remaining and hung on to win 57-54 in the first regular-season game in franchise history.

Just two nights later, the Fever opened its home schedule playing host to the Orlando Miracle. Indiana jumped out to a nine-point halftime lead, but gave up 54 second-half points and lost its opener at Conseco Fieldhouse 88-82 to the Miracle. However, two nights later, the Fever got the chance to pick up its first win at Conseco Fieldhouse against Miami for the second time in four days. The Fever held an eight-point lead at halftime and outscored the Sol 44-31 in the second half, en route to an 80-59 win, for its first win at Conseco Fieldhouse.

After losing the next three games, the Fever got its third win of the season, with a 79-54 victory at Orlando, on June 17. All three of the team's wins came against teams from Florida. The win in Orlando was the Fever's last highlight for several weeks as the next night in Detroit, the team lost its first of 10 straight. Indiana wouldn't win again until July 12.

But, despite the losing streak, Indiana remained close in every game. Several times during the streak, the Fever let wins slip away in the closing seconds. On June 30, against the New York Liberty at Madison Square Garden, the Fever led nearly the entire game, only to see New York take its first lead of the game

as the final buzzer sounded. The Fever lost 72-70 to the Liberty after leading by as many as 18 in the second half.

The very next night at Conseco Fieldhouse, the Fever played host to the Miami Sol — a team it had already beaten twice during the season. But again, a mistake in the closing moments left the Fever with a 54-52 loss. Two nights later at Conseco Fieldhouse, the Fever hosted the Portland Fire, another expansion team, and again came up short, losing 68-64.

On July 8, the Fever played the Phoenix Mercury at Conseco Fieldhouse on NBC, becoming the only expansion team in 2000 to play on national over-the-air television. In a thrilling game, the two teams traded leads the entire second half. With just nine seconds remaining, the Fever's Rita Williams was fouled

and went to the free throw line for two shots with Indiana trailing 66-65. Williams' first free throw rimmed out and she missed the next as the Fever's losing streak grew to 10 games.

However, the very next game Indiana snapped the losing streak with an 81-58 pounding of the Washington Mystics at the MCI Center in Washington, D.C. Williams redeemed herself as she led the Fever in scoring with 17 points and added two rebounds, two assists and four steals. It was especially sweet for Williams as she had been acquired by the Fever in the 2000 WNBA Expansion draft from Washington.

On July 14, the Fever defeated the expansion Seattle Storm 64-45, improving its record to 5-14. The win against Seattle marked the first winning streak in franchise history.

The Fever embarked on its longest road trip of the season when they played the first of five consecutive road games on July 24 in Charlotte. The Fever led by three points with less than 10 seconds remaining, but Charlotte's Andrea Stinson hit a 3-pointer at the buzzer to force the game into overtime. The Sting went on to defeat the Fever in Indiana's only overtime game of the season. The loss at Charlotte was just the first of a long road trip, as the Fever headed for Phoenix the following morning.

On that road trip, Indiana went 1-4, with its only win coming at Portland on July 28. After the 12-day road trip, the Fever had only five games remaining.

But those five games were all to be played in just seven days.

On August 3, at Conseco Fieldhouse, the Fever lost to the Washington Mystics 75-71, falling to 7-21. The following night, the Fever played host to the Cleveland Rockers and improved to 8-21, with an 87-75 victory. The 87 points was the team's highest scoring output for the season. The game also marked the team's first 4-point play in franchise history, when Stephanie McCarty made her free throw after being fouled on a successful 3-point shot.

On August 9, the Fever hosted the Charlotte Sting for the team's final game of the season. Both teams entered the game tied for last place in the WNBA's Eastern Conference, with records of 8-23. The teams had split their previous two contests and a win in the final game of the season would keep either team out of the cellar. Indiana outscored the Sting 30-20 in the second half, building a 17-point lead, and went on to win 61-57 to finish the year at 9-23.

Indianapolis Ice

The 1999-2000 season marked a new era for the Indianapolis Ice. After 11 seasons in the International Hockey League, the Ice changed leagues and owners.

A group of local businessmen, headed by Gary Pedigo, purchased the Ice and moved the team from the IHL to the Central Hockey League. The new ownership and move to the CHL proved very beneficial for the Ice. The team finished second in the Western Conference and won the postseason Miron Cup Championship.

Conseco Fieldhouse was the downtown home to the Ice, hosting eight games during the 1999-2000 season. The Ice finished 6-2 at the Fieldhouse and had an average attendance of 9,200.

The largest crowd to see an Ice game at the Fieldhouse occurred on Feb. 12, when the Ice played the Memphis RiverKings on "Pack The House" Night before 12,979 fans.

The first hockey game at Conseco Fieldhouse featured the Indianapolis Ice vs. San Antonio Iguanas on Saturday, November 20, 1999. The Ice won the game 3-2 before 10,361 cheering fans.

RECORD AT CONSECO FIELDHOUSE: 6-2

Nov. 20	Indianapolis Ice 3 — San Antonio Iguanas 2
Nov. 27	Oklahoma City Blazers 5 — Indianapolis Ice 4
Jan. 15	Indianapolis Ice 6 — Topeka ScareCrows 2
Jan. 22	Indianapolis Ice 4 — San Antonio Iguanas 1
Jan. 25	Idianapolis Ice — Topeka ScareCrows
Feb. 5	Indianapolis Ice 5 — San Antonio Iguanas 4 Shoot Out
Feb. 12	Indianapolis Ice 8 — Memphis RiverKings 3
Feb. 25	Topeka ScareCrows 5 — Indianapolis Ice 2
Feb. 27	Indianapolis Ice 6 — Huntsville Channel Cats 0

Concerts

Bruce Springsteen

NOVEMBER 10, 1999

After being dormant for nearly 10 years, Bruce Springsteen and the E Street Band joined forces and offered the first concert at Conseco Fieldhouse on November 10. The rock 'n' roll legend performed for nearly three hours for the sold out crowd of 18,000.

Dressed in his usual blue jeans and t-shirt, Springsteen belted out all his hits and made the crowd appreciate the "Glory Days" of his music and the excitement of future events at Conseco Fieldhouse.

CLARENCE CLEMONS

Before playing nearly two and one-half hours in front of a sellout crowd, Neil Diamond welcomed the audience and joked, "We've been coming here for 31 years, and they finally put up a new building for us to play in." Diamond thrilled the crowd with his great legacy of songs including: "Hello Again," "Play Me" and "Forever In Blue Jeans," among others. The Neil Diamond concert on December 8 was the first concert performed in the round at Conseco Fieldhouse.

Billy Joel

DECEMBER 14, 1999

John Mellencamp
DECEMBER 31, 1999

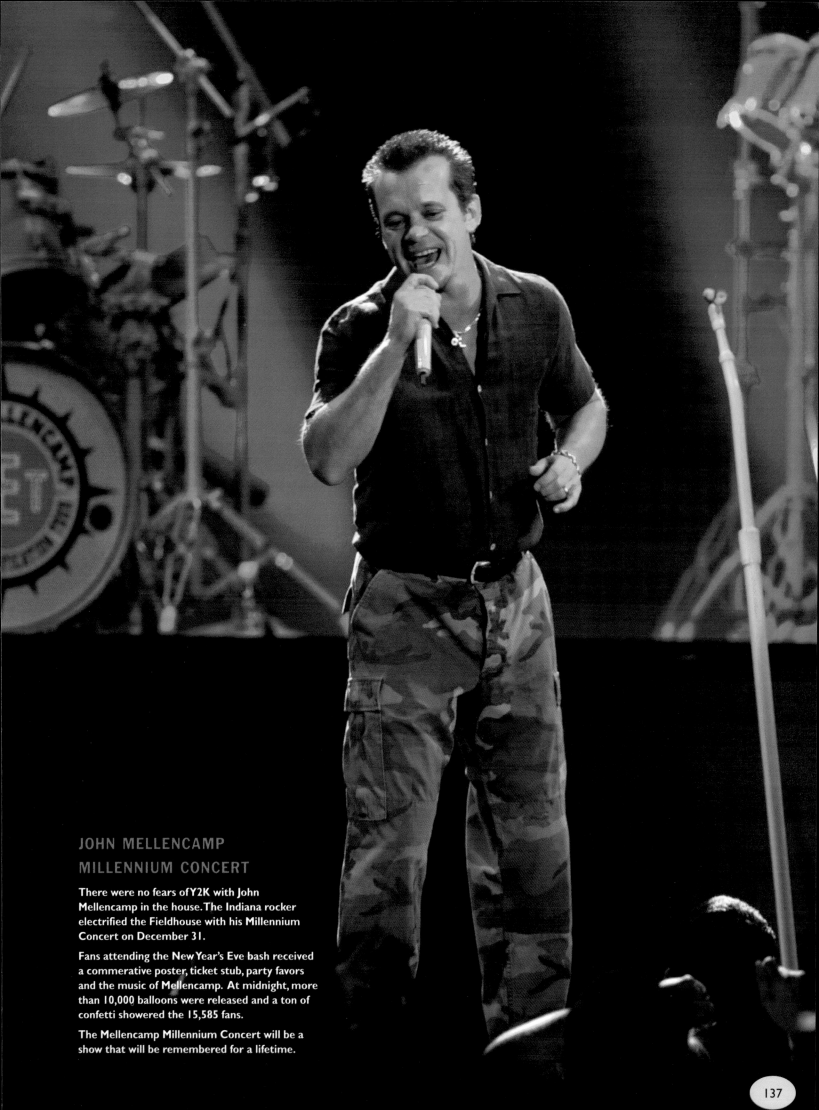

JOHN MELLENCAMP
MILLENNIUM CONCERT

There were no fears of Y2K with John Mellencamp in the house. The Indiana rocker electrified the Fieldhouse with his Millennium Concert on December 31.

Fans attending the New Year's Eve bash received a commerative poster, ticket stub, party favors and the music of Mellencamp. At midnight, more than 10,000 balloons were released and a ton of confetti showered the 15,585 fans.

The Mellencamp Millennium Concert will be a show that will be remembered for a lifetime.

Alan Jackson, with special guest Lonestar, provided music for the first country concert at Conseco Fieldhouse on February 11. Jackson performed a combination of old hits and music from his latest release "Under The Influence," as well as a tribute to Hank Williams.

Alan Jackson
FEBRUARY 11, 2000

The Backstreet Boys

MARCH 10-11, 2000

Teen sensation, The Backstreet Boys, played two sold out concerts on March 10 and 11. One of the most popular groups of the new millennium, these concerts were the fastest to sell out the Fieldhouse. The first show sold out in just eight minutes and both shows were sold out in 18 minutes.

The Backstreet Boys

MARCH 10-11, 2000

The Marsh Holiday Classic was the first high school event in Conseco Fieldhouse. This basketball event featured a tripleheader with two boys games and a girls contest.

Did You Know?

Conseco Fieldhouse contains more than 58,000 square feet of glass.

Kid Rock

DECEMBER 9, 1999

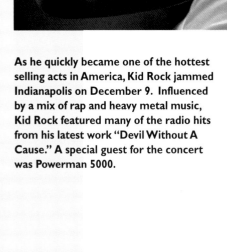

As he quickly became one of the hottest selling acts in America, Kid Rock jammed Indianapolis on December 9. Influenced by a mix of rap and heavy metal music, Kid Rock featured many of the radio hits from his latest work "Devil Without A Cause." A special guest for the concert was Powerman 5000.

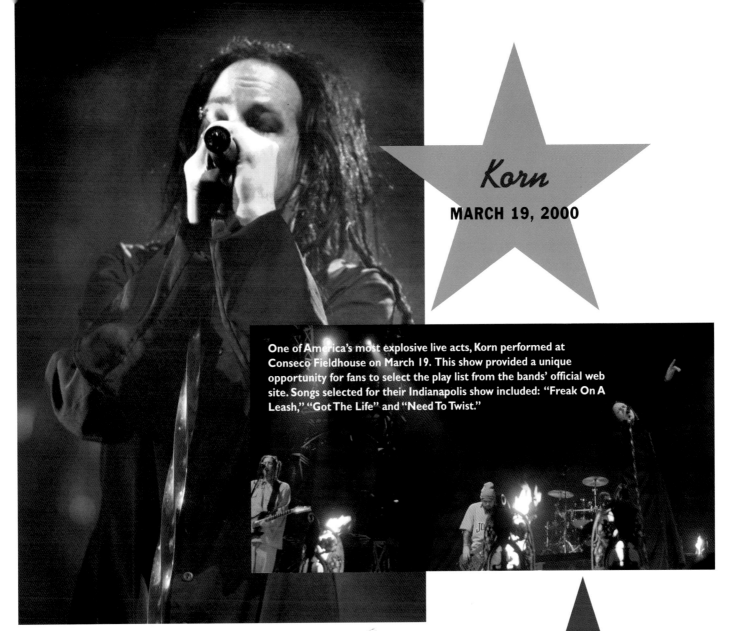

Korn
MARCH 19, 2000

One of America's most explosive live acts, Korn performed at Conseco Fieldhouse on March 19. This show provided a unique opportunity for fans to select the play list from the bands' official web site. Songs selected for their Indianapolis show included: "Freak On A Leash," "Got The Life" and "Need To Twist."

Creed
MARCH 22, 2000

The first band in history to have four No. 1 Rock Radio singles from a debut album, Creed was a hit live, as well. The March 22, Conseco Fieldhouse concert featured their radio chart toppers, including their smash "Higher."

Nine Inch Nails
APRIL 20, 2000

Once a classical pianist, Trent Reznor's discovery of rock music changed his musical direction completely. Reznor, the vocalist and creative force behind Nine Inch Nails, performed with his band at Conseco Fieldhouse on April 20.

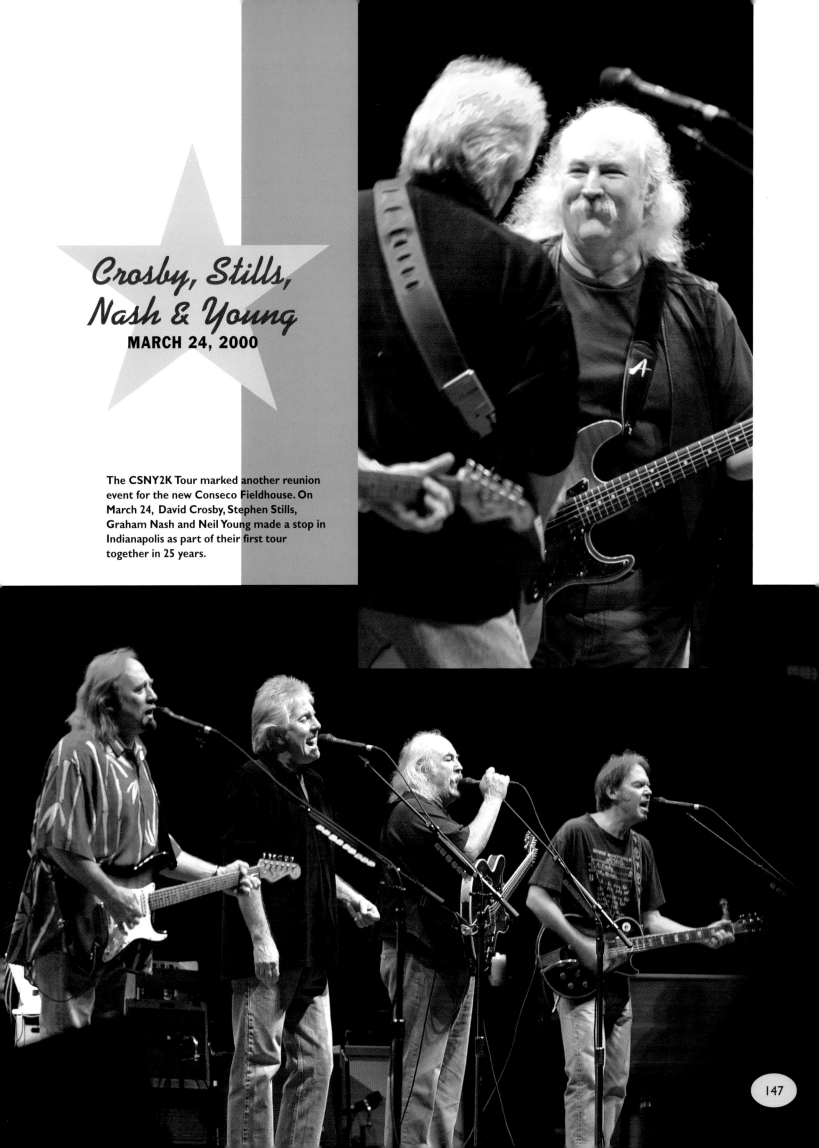

Crosby, Stills, Nash & Young
MARCH 24, 2000

The CSNY2K Tour marked another reunion event for the new Conseco Fieldhouse. On March 24, David Crosby, Stephen Stills, Graham Nash and Neil Young made a stop in Indianapolis as part of their first tour together in 25 years.

The Pacers Fan Jam/ Open House on Sunday, November 7, 1999 attracted over 75,000 visitors in just five hours.

Elton John

APRIL 15, 2000

The "Rocket Man," Elton John, brought his solo acoustic tour to Conseco Fieldhouse on April 15. Accompanied by his piano and a chandelier, the legendary Sir Elton amazed the crowd by performing continuously for three and a half hours.

John showed off his versatility for the 14,792 fans, performing many of his hits such as "Rocket Man," "Bennie and the Jets," "Your Song" and "Goodbye Yellow Brick Road." Interspersed with the classic top 40 hits, John also featured music from his Disney Sound Tracks from Lion King and Eldorado.

Tina Turner
with Lionel Ritchie
MAY 26, 2000

The Twenty Four Seven tour was a live farewell to the arenas and stadiums that Tina Turner filled since her comeback with the 1984 No. I hit single "What's Love Got To Do With It." That year, Tina filled Market Square Arena as a special guest to Lionel Richie. Her May 26 show didn't disappoint with an explosive performance. The show also featured a special treat with Lionel Richie as the opening act — a reversal of their billing from the '84 show.

151

Ricky Martin

JULY 5, 2000

Special Event Facts

The first (non-Pacers) sporting event at Conseco Fieldhouse was WCW Monday Night Nitro on November 8, 1999.

An enthusiastic crowd danced the night away with Ricky Martin on July 5. Opening the show with "Livin' La Vida Loca," fans remained on their feet ready to "Shake Their Bon Bon" throughout the show.

Up in Smoke Concert

JUNE 30, 2000

It was every rapper's dream during the hip-hop extravaganza of the "Up In Smoke" Tour on June 30. The royal court of rap took center stage with Dr. Dre, Snoop Dogg, Ice Cube, Eminem and Warren G.

As part of the annual Indiana Black Expo festivities, the Music Heritage Festival was a two-day event at the Field-house on July 15-16. Earth, Wind & Fire headlined the first night concert, with special guest Teena Marie. Day two featured Frankie Beverley & Maze, Gerald LeVert, K-Ci & Jo Jo, and Indianapolis native Kevon Edmonds.

AC/DC

AUGUST 27, 2000

Legendary rock group AC/DC went on tour for the first time in over five years and featured an August 27 stop in Indianapolis. Fans were treated to the pulsating rock beat of "Shook Me All Night Long" and "Back in Black."

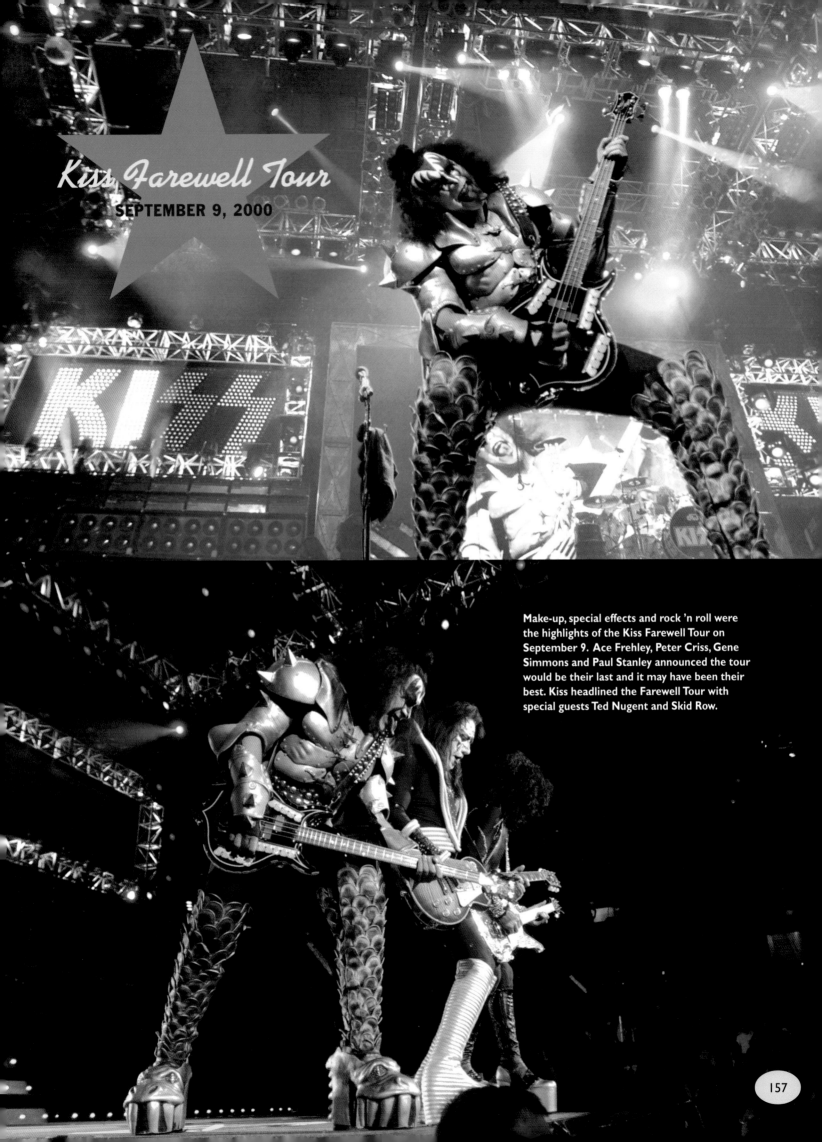

Kiss Farewell Tour
SEPTEMBER 9, 2000

Make-up, special effects and rock 'n roll were the highlights of the Kiss Farewell Tour on September 9. Ace Frehley, Peter Criss, Gene Simmons and Paul Stanley announced the tour would be their last and it may have been their best. Kiss headlined the Farewell Tour with special guests Ted Nugent and Skid Row.

*Faith Hill &
Tim McGraw*

SEPTEMBER 22, 2000

One of the hottest tickets of the year was for the "Soul 2 Soul" tour, featuring Tim McGraw and Faith Hill. The husband and wife team split time on stage performing solo, then finished as a duet. The September 22 show was one of the most exciting and visually stimulating tours of its kind.

Top ranked 4A Lady Giants of Ben Davis played No. 1 3A Cathedral Irish in the first high school event at Conseco Fieldhouse. This was the first of three games for the Marsh High School Holiday Classic. Chesterton played LaPorte and Jeffersonville battled Muncie Central in the boys games.

Dixie Chicks
OCTOBER 22, 2000

Packing a banjo, fiddle and crystal-clear vocals, The Dixie Chicks showed why they had been honored with the Country Music Association's Group of the Year Award. The Dixie Chicks performed on October 22, with special guest Ricky Skaggs.

'N Sync

OCTOBER 25 & 26, 2000

Pop phenomenon, 'N Sync, closed out the first year of events at Conseco Fieldhouse with concerts on October 25 and 26. What better way to say "Bye, Bye, Bye" to the inaugural year than with one of the major players in the world of pop music and their No Strings Attached Tour.

Special Events

Bill Cosby
NOVEMBER 14, 1999

One of America's favorite storytellers and stand-up comedians, Bill Cosby brought his humor to Conseco Fieldhouse on November 14. This was the closing act to the week-long activities for the Fieldhouse Grand Opening.

MICHAEL FLATLEY'S
Lord of the Dance
JANUARY 27, 2000

Michael Flatley's Lord of the Dance featured a variety of high-energy, foot-stomping dance styles centered around a Celtic musical theme. Complete with lighting and stage effects that hinted of Las Vegas, this January 27 show amazed the Conseco Fieldhouse audience.

The first college event at Conseco Fieldhouse was the Purdue Blockbuster Classic on December 18. The Lady Boilers played Kentucky in the first game and the Purdue Men's team played Ball State.

Luciano Pavarotti

FEBRUARY 20, 2000

Opera legend Luciano Pavarotti made Conseco Fieldhouse part of his limited 2000 American Tour on February 20. It was only his second concert in the Circle City, the last coming in January, 1986.

The Maestro was accompanied by the Indianapolis Chamber Orchestra and joined on his duets with Miss Annalisa Raspagliosi.

Boston Pops
MARCH 28, 2000

Conductor Keith Lockhart and the Boston Pops provided a Celtic Celebration on March 28. The orchestra, along with Irish Dancers and a bagpipe soloist, entertained the audience with selections from "Riverdance," "Braveheart" and "Rob Roy."

Family Events

Harlem Globetrotters

DECEMBER 29, 1999
APRIL 1, 2000

It was high-flying slam-dunking excitement with the outrageously funny Harlem Globetrotters on December 29. The "Ambassadors of Goodwill" showed they could do more than clown around in a second visit to Conseco Fieldhouse on April 1.

In a no-nonsense, competitive game, The Globetrotters defeated the College All-Stars, 82-80, in the National Association of Basketball Coaches (NABC) Roundball Challenge.

WCW

NOVEMBER 8, 1999
JULY 30, 2000

World Championship Wrestling's Monday Night Nitro was part of the Conseco Fieldhouse Opening Week events on November 8. This was one of two visits by WCW, with the second event falling on July 30.

The World Wrestling Federation made two stops at Conseco Fieldhouse during the inaugural year. The first (scheduled for January 28) was rescheduled for March 8, due to poor weather. The March 8 show was followed by WWF's Raw Is War on May 22.

A host of wrestlers were part of these events, including one of WWF's most popular wrestlers "The Rock." During Raw Is War, "The Rock" was part of the main event, teaming up with Kane and the Pall Bearer to battle Triple H and XPAC.

WWF
MARCH 8, 2000
MAY 22, 2000

Disney on Ice
75th Anniversary Show
DECEMBER 2-5, 1999

The largest crowd to see an Ice game at Conseco Fieldhouse during it's first year was 12,979 on February 12, 2000. The Ice played the Memphis Riverkings on "Pack The House Night."

Disney's "75th Anniversary Show" was the first family show featured at Conseco Fieldhouse and ran December 2-5. The Disney cast of characters, lead by Mickey and Minnie Mouse, performed seven shows during their four-day adventure.

Target Stars on Ice
FEBRUARY 6, 2000

Both "Target Stars On Ice" and "Champions on Ice" included Conseco Fieldhouse on their 2000 tours. Similar in theme, each show featured a cast of world and Olympic skating champions.

Champions on Ice
APRIL 18, 2000

"Target Stars On Ice" appeared on February 6, with Tara Lipinski, Kristi Yamaguchi, Scott Hamilton and Kurt Browning.

The "Champions On Ice" show on April 18, was highlighted by performances from Michelle Kwan, Nicole Bobek, Brian Boitano and Victor Petrenko.

Prince of Wales Band

OCTOBER 24, 2000

Bagpipes, drums and Highland Dancers provided the sites and sounds of Blackwatch and the Prince of Wales Band. The October 24 concert featured the music of Scotland, England, Ireland and Wales.

Ringling Bros. and Barnum & Bailey Circus
SEPTEMBER 27–OCTOBER 1, 2000

The 129th edition of Ringling Bros. and Barnum & Bailey Circus featured a five-day, eight-show performance from September 27 – October 1. "The Greatest Show On Earth" mesmerized its fans with the "Living Carousel" and over 10,000 lights. Along with the usual hilarious antics of the circus clowns, daring motorcyclists risked their lives in the "Globe of Death."

Other Sporting Events

Circle City
Grand National Rodeo
JANUARY 7-9, 2000

The Circle City Grand National Rodeo made a three-day stop to Conseco Fieldhouse on January 7-9. It was the first event that required dirt in order to have a competition. Five professional events were featured: bareback bronc riding, saddle bronc riding, steer wrestling, calf roping, and the crowd favorite — bull riding.

Indiana University continued their winning ways during the Hoosier Classic on December 27 and 28. Led by seniors A. J. Guyton and Michael Lewis, the Hoosiers easily defeated Canisius University, 95-53, and won the championship over Holy Cross, 79-44.

Hoosier Classic
DECEMBER 27-28, 1999

Purdue University found Conseco Fieldhouse a mixed bag as far as home-court advantage in the annual Blockbuster Classic. The men's team lost to Ball State, 72-52, while the Lady Boilers opened the classic with a victory over the University of Kentucky, 48-40.

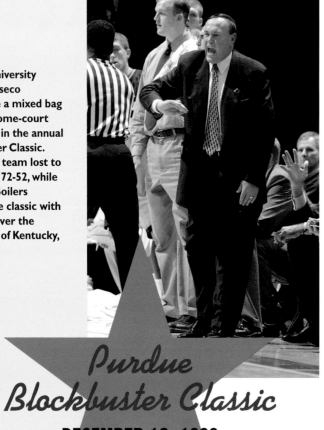

Purdue Blockbuster Classic
DECEMBER 18, 1999

Big Ten Women's Tournament

MARCH 2-5, 2000

Over 1,461,359 man hours were spent on the construction of Conseco Fieldhouse.

The first postseason basketball event of any kind at Conseco Fieldhouse took place on March 2-5, as the Big Ten Women's Basketball Tournament came to town. This 10-game, single-elimination tournament featured all 11 conference schools, with the winner earning an automatic bid to the NCAA tournament.

Katie Douglas scored 24 points, as the Purdue Lady Boilers knocked off top-seeded Penn State, 71-63, for the championship. The victory marked the first time in Big Ten Women's history that a team won back-to-back-to-back tournament titles.

NCAA Weekend

MARCH 30–APRIL 2, 2000

Indianapolis was the home of college basketball's 2000 Final Four, and Conseco Fieldhouse hosted many of the ancillary events. The weekend kicked off with ESPN's Slam Dunk & Three Point Shootout on March 30. Collegiate all-stars, including Indiana's A.J. Guyton, participated in the events.

During the slam dunk events, celebrity judges, including the Indiana Pacers' Austin Croshere and Derrick McKey, were part of the festivities, as well as ESPN broadcaster Dick Vitale.

The National Association of Basketball Coaches also held its All-Star Game during Final Four weekend, featuring collegiate all-stars vying against the Harlem Globetrotters on April 1.

On April 2, it was the high schoolers' turn, as high school all-stars took center stage against an international all-star team in the Nike International Hoop Summit. Among members on the U.S. High School Basketball team were Indiana's own Jared Jeffries (Bloomington North) and Zach Randolph (Marion High School).

183

DECEMBER 22, 1999

The inaugural year of Conseco Fieldhouse provided fans a variety of high school events. The first such event was the Marsh High School Holiday Basketball Classic on December 22. This basketball tripleheader featured both boys and girls competition from around the state. Tipping off the Marsh Classic were two undefeated, No. 1 ranked teams — the Lady Giants of Ben Davis and Cathedral's Lady Irish. The boys' games featured a Duneland Conference battle with LaPorte and Chesterton, followed by the Jeffersonville Red Devils and Muncie Central Bearcats.

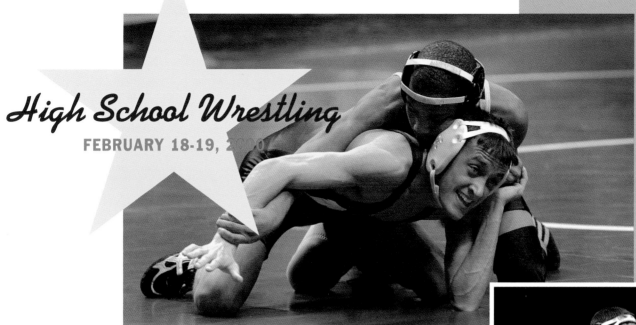

High School Wrestling
FEBRUARY 18-19, 2000

On February 18-19, the Indiana High School Athletic Association (IHSAA) hosted its State Wrestling Finals. The two-day tournament provided a state champion in each of the 14 weight classes.

State champions were crowned in basketball on March 25 during the IHSAA Boys Finals. Each class of basketball had its own champion. In the 4A Finals, Marion defeated Bloomington North, 62-56; in the 3A Finals, Indianapolis Brebeuf defeated Gary Andrean, 72-56; in the 2A Finals Westview defeated Winchester, 59-53; and in the 1A Finals, Lafayette Central Catholic defeated Union (Dugger), 80-72.

State Finals
MARCH 25, 2000

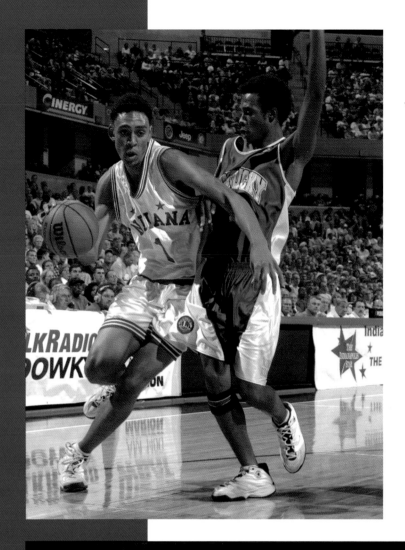

On June 24, the boys and girls all-star teams from Indiana showed their dominance in basketball over the Blue Grass State with a sweep in the annual Indiana-Kentucky All-Star Game.

Roy Jones, Jr.
Boxing
MAY 13, 2000

A landmark event in the history of Indiana sports took place on May 13, with the largest boxing event in the state. The event truly lived up to its billing as "The Greatest Fighter Fighting at the Greatest Sports Facility."

In the co-featured bout, Bernard Hopkins put his IBF title on the line against Syd Vanderpool. Both fights were part of a nationally televised feature on HBO Sports.

Known as the best pound-for-pound
fighter in the world, Roy Jones Jr.,
defended his light heavyweight title
against the WBA's No.1 contender,
Richard Hall.